Each Writes of Passage

a collaboration

by

Gary Bacon Ph. D.

and

the students of

The Learning Community

Published by

Rainbow Bridge, Palo Alto, California

Each Writes of Passage
a collaboration by
Gary Bacon
and the students of
The Learning Community

Published by:
Rainbow Bridge
823 Forest Avenue
Palo Alto, CA 94301

Other Rainbow Bridge books:

ESSENTIAL EDUCATION: Drawing Forth the Golden Child
by Gary Bacon, Ph.D.

journey to the heart: Capturing the Spirit of Global Education
by The Learning Community

About the cover:
Artwork by Janna Mordan, a former Learning Community student. Janna created the image for a group project that she had helped lead while in The Learning Community. She was inspired by the depth of support and sharing within the group that gave its members the strength to grow, to take interpersonal risks, to inquire, and to create.

Dedication:

We wish to dedicate this book to those people who have the vision and the fortitude to make the process of education an instrument of transformation. We acknowledge the educator who captures the moment that lies between *what was* and *what is to be* and helps transform that moment into excitement and inspiration. We honor the parent who patterns his or her life energy around the holistic development of the child. We applaud the efforts of the student who is able to develop an awareness of the higher purpose of education and who demands to play an active role in its fulfillment.

Table of Contents

Acknowledgments

This project has been a collaboration in the truest sense of the word. Over thirty people have made some form of contribution to the final product that lies between the covers of this book. The initial idea grew out of the co-created learning experience of the students in the 1993-94 Learning Community. The idea took form and evolved over time as new people rose to the occasion to help shepherd the concept to completion. The students who initiated the writing project lived it. They committed their energy to create an interdisciplinary studies program that honored the individual, empowered the group, and contributed to the world. Then they chose to write about their individual and group experiences as part of their curriculum. Their energy fueled the project and guaranteed it success. Without their commitment to create value in their lives and in their education, the project would not have had the spark to endure. The students were:

Tamika Austin	Paula Martinez	Andy Press
Mike Britton	Andrea Meyer	Jenny Salinas
Victor Enciso	Janna Mordan	Wendy Salinas
Joe George	Kristie Nelson	Joanna Scripps
Alma Hernandez	Brenda Nuñez	Greg Smith
Shawn Hescock	Mitchie Padaong	Garrett West
Paki Kasle-Muthig	Evan Peterson	

When our time frame extended past the end of the school year and into the summer, a small group of students stayed with the project. They deserve special thanks. Joe, Andrea, Janna, Evan, and Jenny spent several weeks editing the papers that the group had written. The process was not easy; our group had generated volumes of paper and the editors were challenged to direct the divergent topics into one coherent work. The editors were unable to complete the work and the project lay fallow for almost a year. Without the summer effort, however, the whole project may have stopped.

Another group resurrected the project one year later. This time Tamika, Joe, Paki, Kristie, Jenny, and Greg were joined by Adrienne Ratner and Angel Burgess from the 1994-95 Learning Community. Gary had just returned from a visit to Xalapa, Mexico, from which he gained new inspiration for the project and a more coherent vision for its implementation. The group concurred with the new direction and met throughout the summer to discuss the details and to respond to oral readings of new and revised papers. This group chose to use the lives of nine students—Tamika, Jeremy Tobin, Greg, Shawn, Jenny, Kristie, Angel, Janna, and Adrienne—to characterize The Learning Community's transformational process. As the summer ended, the group disbanded as most of the students went back to their jobs or college. Once again, the project went through a nine-month incubation period.

The final phase of the project started in June of 1996. Gary worked with each person whose life experiences were associated with each chapter of the book. Some of the chapters needed editing; others needed major rewrites and transitions; others needed to be written. Gary assisted in the re-writes and, in some passages, reconstructed or completed the entire chapter. He enlisted student help wherever possible and conducted extensive interviews with the students and their families. Atanacio and Eugenia Salinas and Betty Burgess generously shared their family memories and their living rooms with Gary. Kris Mordan read Janna's passage and made helpful suggestions.

Many people provided valuable help in the final editing process. Adrienne Ratner fully committed her editing talent and her philosophical insights throughout the final phase as well as writing her passage. Leticia Burton provided helpful consultations on passages one and seven. Dave Muffly edited and consulted on passage six. Hobson Bryan read the work-in-progress and made useful suggestions that could be applied globally. Trude Hoffacker took time out of her first year of retirement as an English teacher to edit. Charles Tipps helped fine-tune the final work. Cynde AvéLallemant created the layout and the color separations for the cover. Carmen Gómez was a constant source of inspiration, support, editing, advice, and patience throughout the project.

A special thanks is due The Community Foundation of Santa Clara County and those who assisted in the pre-sale efforts for helping fund the first printing of this book.

Beyond all other efforts, the courage, the hard work, and the dedication of the students of The Learning Community over its twenty-five year history made this book possible.

Forethought

My work in education has spanned four decades. The teachers that taught me had survived the Great Depression and two world wars. They were a rare breed of human beings. Their character was forged from life events which set them apart from most people in education today. I know that I was a recipient of an excellent education. I learned about the world from these people. Yet I always felt that there was something missing in my educational experience.

It is claimed that people who choose the teaching profession either *loved* or *hated* their schooling. I don't think it would be fair to say that I hated school; on the contrary, it was the place in which I met other kids my age and learned the process of socialization. However, for my kind of personality and learning style, I didn't really find a compelling attraction to my K-12 schooling. Perhaps for this reason I became a teacher. I wanted to help make education more personal, more interactive, and more focused on meaning.

I began my career in a rural community in southwestern Montana. Students came to our school from as far away as seventy miles. The country was big, rugged, and treacherous in the winter months. I taught five different classes over three grade levels and didn't have the luxury of time to criticize the system for its inadequacies. I was in survival mode trying to teach math, science, biology, social studies, and even Montana History. By the nature of the time and the location, the only option was to be personal, interactive, and focused on meaning. When one is surrounded by the most beautiful displays of land and life and the most unpredictable whims of nature, life takes on a personal relevance that is undeniable.

Something was stirring inside me, though. I seemed compelled to move on. It was as though I was being pushed by my past or summoned by my future, all at the same times. After five years of teaching in Montana, I moved to California. My explanation at the time was that I had "itchy feet." Perhaps it was my soul that was "itchy." In any case, I arrived in California in the mid-Sixties, a time of great social turbulence. Even my early days of white-water river-rafting in Montana seemed to pale in comparison to the turbulent sea of social protest that I encountered in my new home.

At twenty-eight years old, I waded into this turbulent sea of social protest and psychological soul searching—I'm glad that I did. I experienced personal intimacy and camaraderie like I had never experienced before. I became immersed in a sea of social questioning, interaction, and change. I was confronted, full bore, with personal and social meaning. I felt alive and I wanted to make sure that, while I was still in touch with this intense sense of purpose, I could somehow translate the essence of this feeling into my professional work. I wanted to make my life and my teaching exist as one reality and strove to remove the artificial barriers that I felt were lodged between me and my work.

I remember walking into the City Lights bookstore in San Francisco in the late Sixties. The store was owned by beat poet Lawrence Ferlingetti. I picked up one of Ferlingetti's books of poetry, *The Coney Island of the Mind*, and opened it to a random passage. I found a passage that implored the reader to "hang your necktie on a lamp post." It spoke of shedding social convention in order to make contact with reality, which the modern, impersonal world was leaving behind. I thought back to my early years of attending school and my recent years of teaching. The isolation that I felt and the isolation that I was perpetuating in the classroom almost overwhelmed me at that moment. Over the next few weeks, that experience provided me with new symbolism to ponder, even as I dressed in the uniform of my profession as I readied myself for my teaching day.

Over time, the necktie came off, but there was more to that fashion change than shedding symbols. I had to transform my teaching and my approach to life to begin my search for real meaning. I found myself in a world that I didn't know. All the old conventions and formulas didn't seem to work.

I was treading on a road that was not charted or certain, and probably as frightening as it was exciting.

My questioning and experimenting took me away from the certainties of teaching science and mathematics on which I had come to rely. I was intrigued by the mysteries of the mind and the vastness of the terrain of the human psyche. Although those interests led me eventually to graduate work in Transpersonal Psychology, they did not lead me away from teaching.

Then, twenty-five years ago, in the midst of the social and political chaos of the late Sixties and early Seventies, I had a rare opportunity to work with a grass-roots group who came together to create an alternative to traditional education. The group—consisting of parents, students, teachers, and others in our community—developed a proposal for a more open, hands-on, student-oriented process of education. The program, The Learning Community, was implemented in our public school and became an ongoing laboratory of experimentation and change for my students and me.

My experience, as the guardian of the program, has been rich. On one hand, I have had to bolster the program from the sometimes whimsical, sometimes fickle trends of education in order to insure the program's survival. On the other hand, I have been able to help the program evolve, unencumbered by the slow and sometimes arduous pace of change that often chokes the life out of the public school system.

Those of us who proposed the program established a system that is regenerative each year and that, therefore, engages the learner in a yearly re-creation of its form and content. It is no wonder that such a program would touch the lives of its students in ways that are personal, interactive, and focused on meaning. This book offers a glimpse of how the process of education in The Learning Community has transformed the lives of nine young people in their quest for learning.

We have woven three strands of life development—the personal, the interpersonal, and the institutional— into each chapter (or "passage" as we have called them here). We share archetypal stories of young people who are growing up in today's world. We share how young people, coming from diverse backgrounds, can join others to create a community of learners who care about each other and who want to make a difference in the world. We document the progression of the life-changing experience that we have observed in an educational community.

Our specific classroom events and goals vary greatly each year depending on the teacher's and students' vision—especially as the class interrelates with the political and ecological events in the world. Yet, underlying each of these very unique yearly experiences lies a fundamental transformative process that has the potential of becoming the students' *rite of passage*. We invite you to share our lives and experiences as we seek to understand the inherent process that guides our educational experience.

Gary Bacon

Each Writes of Passage

Passage One:
Finding a Family

The Beat of the Distant Drum

Tamika

My grandmother tells me that I have two lines of ancestry. Both of them have etched my character; both have left a distinct sound in my heart, a constant, driving beat, much like the beat of a drum. The drum, the rhythmic beat of an ancient drum, has always been my sanctuary when the world around me seems to close in and I am about to abandon hope. When I sit alone and close my eyes, I can feel the deep beat inside me—steady, strong, and full of meaning and history. Sometimes I have felt that it is the only connection I have with my past; all else has been erased.

I was born into an imperfect world. I was thrust into a family that was bruised. Our family consisted of my mother and my seven brothers and sisters—from four different men. I was the sixth child and, by the time I was born, my mother was with another man. I never had someone that I could call a father, just a man I never knew. My mother did her best to survive, but as the men in her life moved on, we were left with another brother or sister, a mother deeper in despair, and a life with no one to look up to, no money, and no promise of a future.

My mother died when I was only seven years old. I didn't know what death was; I saw everyone crying, so I cried too. I just thought that that was what you were supposed to do when people died. Later, when I realized that she wasn't coming back, I was devastated. My mother would never be here again to kiss me, hug me, or let me sleep with her when I was scared. I remember pretending to be scared so that I could sleep with her. Now I *was scared* but I would never be able to get in bed with her again.

I felt abandoned and alone. Years later, I was able to express my feelings in a poem.

> *Mothers Don't:*
> Mothers don't leave you alone
> at night to cry yourself to sleep;
> they don't leave you to wallow
> in the hole of pain they dug so deep.

Mothers don't send you away
when they don't want you any more;
they aren't supposed to scream
and yell, then throw you out the door.

Mothers don't tell you they love
you as a form of punishment;
instead it is supposed to delight you
like a bird that heaven sent.

Mothers don't leave you at the tender age
of seven to cook and prepare your own meals;
instead they should care only about
what you think and how you feel.

Mothers don't discipline you
for something you haven't done;
they don't make a difference
between their daughter or their son.

Mothers don't push you away when
you need a soft kiss or a warm hug;
they're suppose to wrap you up
and keep you safe and snug.

Mothers don't let you go around
with dirty clothes and ragged sleeve;
Mothers don't close their eyes on you
but most of all, Mothers don't leave.

Tears weren't helpful either. My cries for help were answered by a hollow emptiness, followed by sadness, more sadness, and more emptiness. The drum seemed so faint now. I wasn't so sure that I could even hear a distant drum.

The State wanted my twin brothers and me—we were the youngest kids—to live with our fathers, but the men could not be found; I don't think they wanted to be found. We had a desperate need to live somewhere, so we were separated and placed with foster families. We wanted to be together and our prayers were answered when my grandmother arranged for us to move to California to be with her.

When we got to move in with our grandmother, we became a family again. Oh, how I could hear the drums when grandma held me real close to her chest; my heart seemed to flutter when I hugged her back, not wanting to let go.

My grandmother says that I am a descendant of a proud tribe of West Africans who lived somewhere in the Congo Basin. They lived a simple, yet peaceful, existence that depended on a harmonious relationship with the land and the water and the cycles of life. My ancestors developed this way of life thousands and thousands of years ago by adapting to change in the environment and making friends with the forces of nature and by learning to work together with their brothers and sisters. There was a clear voice within these people, an ancient soul that bridged time. The voice bore the accumulated inner wisdom of the time in which they arose from ancient bones, somewhere in the heart of Africa.

My grandmother enrolled me in the neighborhood school. It was tough, but I made it through with the help of my fourth-grade teacher, Mrs. Kaje-Weng. She was amazing, so caring and giving. She taught me so much about living in the world and taking care of life. She saw all of life as being precious, especially, it seemed to me, mine. She helped me get through some terrible times. I didn't know at the time that she would be such an important person in my life.

Unfortunately, my family life with my grandmother didn't last for long. When I was eleven, she had a stroke and died. The beat almost died with her. I was used to caring for my brothers, but we were separated again. I felt that I had lost everything. I went to live with my aunt and her family. I felt like I was a cloud of disruption to them; my time with them lasted only for eight months. After that, I was sent back to Chicago.

Finally, my brothers and I were placed in foster families. We were caught in the system, and, while we had food, clothing, and a roof over our heads, we didn't have family. We never had a dad, mom was dead, and now we were split up. I felt lonelier than ever. I lived with a foster family for the next two-and-a-half years. That worked out for a while, until the man tried to molest me. When I refused to cooperate with him and complained about it, the family didn't want me anymore. I had to leave and become a ward of the court until I was assigned to live with my older sister, Sarah.

As I suffered through the ordeal of changing households, I found some comfort in my natural talents. I choreographed my own dances. When I lived with my younger brothers I involved them. We laughed and danced and played for hours. I always loved to move with the beat, and sometimes I spent hours in my room dancing. I really didn't want to drown in my situation. I liked things upbeat, so I always walked into a quiet room, even at school, and said loudly "Good morning, everybody!" It usually worked; the energy rose immediately.

Sure, I had my dark days, days that I just wanted to stay in bed and hide under the covers. And I had a temper, but I had to go inside myself with it because there was no way to work it out in the world. If someone came down on me in a negative way, I'd get really pissed and go inside. It wasn't always safe to show my anger outwardly. But most of the time, I'd just use my talents to get other people up.

When Sarah took me in, it was a homecoming, to some extent. Once again, I got to live with my younger brothers and my older sister and brother. But, by now, I was afraid to hope for much. I was a fourteen-year-old girl with the responsibility of taking care of myself in the home. Now I had to take care of myself on the streets of Chicago as well.

One cold winter day in March, I woke up at the usual time for school. I am not a morning person, so I hesitated for a while before I actually got up. Finally, I rolled out of bed and went to the bathroom. Inside, I sighed as I looked at the job ahead of me in the mirror. I almost cried realizing how long it would take to make my hair look halfway decent. Not stressing too much, because it was a Friday, I went ahead and got dressed. As usual, I was the only one awake in the house; I knew I didn't have time for breakfast, so I grabbed my backpack and keys, then ran for the door.

Outside, the morning air was still brisk. Although there was no snow on the ground, I could still feel the piercing Chicago wind blowing down my neck. Pulling my jacket closer around me, I walked towards the bus stop.

Every day it depressed me more and more to see the streets that my friends and I lived on—the vacant lots filled with trash, the train tracks scarred with graffiti, the homeless sleeping in doorways, and the drug dealers up early knowing that their customers had been waiting for them. These and all the other signs of poverty stared me in the face as I walked down the familiar, well-populated street that led me to a refuge, the safe haven that school was supposed to provide.

Thousands of thoughts filled my mind as I made my way across the street. Lifting my head to look down the alley as I passed, I made sure there were no cars rushing through to the street. I heard footsteps and I felt the presence of a person walking behind me. Nervousness built up inside of me. I started to pick up the pace when a male voice said, "Hi," and asked me my name.

I turned just enough to see the face belonging to the voice and relaxed a little. It was not uncommon for guys to try to talk to any girl they saw, so thinking that was all there was to it, I prepared myself to give him the "I'm not interested" talk. That plan backfired because he didn't stop talking and asking questions. I thought I might try a different tactic and tried to cross the street. That escape faded when my uninvited escort told me not to move or my head would be blown off.

At that moment my jaw dropped, as did my heart. I realized that the man was a criminal and I was being added to his list of victims. I swallowed hard while the tears rolled down my face. Unconsciously, I followed the commands that were given to me in a steady stream. Even though the sun was shining, everything started to get dark before my eyes. He told me to walk down steps that led into the entryway of the basement beneath the porch of a vacant building. There I stood wanting to plead, scream, and pray that he would not go through with his crime, but the sight of the gun kept all my emotions inside. He told me to remove my clothes. I hesitated until he reinforced his statement by pointing his "steel manhood" at me. He pulled me down onto the cold cement. The cement reflected the coldness of his heart and the feeling that gradually overcame me. I cried softly as I lay there unwillingly having my sacred pureness taken away from me.

When I was finally released, I ran so fast I hardly remember running back home. I knocked on the door of our second-floor apartment. I was out of breath. I could see the look of wonder on my sister's face as I walked back in the door. Tears were streaming down my face while I tried to tell her why I wasn't at school. Somehow I managed to get across to her that I had been violated in the worst way. Instantly, pain washed over her face. She grabbed me, hugged me, and we cried together. Since we didn't have a telephone, we went upstairs to use our neighbor's. Hysterical and hyperventilating, I sat down to be comforted by our neighbor, Barbara, while my sister made the call to the police.

Curled up on the couch, I lay there and waited for the commotion to start. The trauma played over and over in my mind. I pictured a tall, stern police detective with broad shoulders standing over me. Cold and distant from his work, he would talk to me and ask me what had happened. When the officers arrived, the man fit my expectation. Seeing the small, kind-looking woman officer who accompanied him gave me a little comfort. They both bent down so that they could talk to me. The male officer tried to be gentle, but he could tell how hard it was for me to respond to him. I tried with all my might to tell the story calmly, but the tears would not stop. After a long struggle, we got through it and then headed for the hospital.

I was frightened by the white, busy, sterile hospital. I knew pain and death lurked around every door; this was the place my family members had come to die. My case was an emergency, so I was taken in right away. They took me to a room that contained a table with paper sheets covering it. It was like most of the medical rooms that I had been in. The only difference was that the table had a place where the feet were supposed to go. As usual, I was told to undress, but this time the nurse didn't leave the room. With her glove-covered hands, she picked up my underwear and stuffed it inside a plastic bag. She told me it would be tested and that I would have to leave it there. After undressing, I lay back on the table and waited.

The doctor entered the room and smiled at me. In a calm, professional voice he asked me how old I was. I told him I was fourteen; he frowned and sadly shook his head as if he could see his own child lying there. He put his latex gloves on and told me to place my feet on each of the two metal stirrups. Before I could fully grasp what would happen to me, everything was done. I remember cold instruments, poking, scraping, and sticking. I know he told me what he was going to do, but it didn't quite register in my mind. After the tests, I was left feeling like a gum wrapper thrown away after the important part was taken out. The new detectives, who came in next, didn't help much either. Their line of questioning left me drained and empty as if I were the carcass remaining after the vultures' feast.

I became more frustrated and angry as each detective demanded that I repeat my story. My feelings had no where to go, they just piled up like dirty laundry. After a while I wished I were a part of that pile, for I was in desperate need of being clean. I didn't want to remember, yet I was forced to relive the pain each time they made me repeat my ordeal. I felt myself drifting in and out of reality, confusing myself with my own words. Trying desperately to keep my story the same every time, I searched my mind to find the words and phrases I had just used. The questions that I was asked seemed to get more unfamiliar, and I wasn't sure how to answer them. I could hear myself responding; I felt awkward and unclear. I was getting closer and closer to feeling as if I was going to explode. Finally, the sense of tightness was released when they told me that I could go. I was left with a hollow and empty feeling—not even a hint of a drum sounded inside me.

The doctor came back into the room to give me medication and tell my sister what kind of care I needed. After he gave us his heart-felt advice, he asked us to fill out report forms in the waiting room. I was exhausted and I had an incredible headache. A huge gray cloud filled with all the disgusting things that I had been through, rested on my shoulders and stretched out above me. I wondered how I would get through the next hour, then the next day, and then the rest of my life. I tried to cry, but the tears were stuck inside. When we reached home, I looked out the window and searched for a place to go. Everything I saw made me realize home was the one and only place that I had. And yet, no where, not even in that apartment, did I feel like I was at home.

> *I remember my grandmother's stories and often think of my ancestors. My ancestors were ripped from their homes in Africa and brought to the "New World" as a "cash crop" by the "civilized" races of Europe. After serving the agricultural aristocracy of the Old South for two hundred years, people like my ancestors were "freed." Some of the former slaves stayed in the rural South and worked land owned by white people. Others traveled west in search of their own land or north where they became the underclass of the industrial age. My grandparents joined others who flocked to the big industrial cities of the North during World War II to find a home in places like Chicago.*

I often wondered if the rapist was to blame or if I, too, was at fault. Society wants us to blame someone; because I didn't know him or understand why this had happened, I blamed myself. For a long time I went around with this thought taped to my forehead. If it wasn't my fault, why did I have to walk the same streets every morning to get to school? And if it wasn't my fault, how come nothing changed and I received help only that one day? Counseling was prescribed, but counseling was never received; when you are poor, counseling isn't an option. I felt trapped in an endless cycle of coldness, coldness that enveloped me and crept inside. Nothing could affect me nor could anyone make me believe that I didn't deserve the hand that life had dealt out to me.

I didn't really see what was going on until I was taken out of the situation. I know now that, as a woman, my world is similar to other woman's. What happened to me can happen anywhere and to anyone. It took me a long time to realize there is no in-depth selection process in crime. I did nothing wrong. The only problem lay within the heart and mind of the man who took that precious part of my body away from me. I will never know what train of thought led him to his decision, and I really don't want to know. I guess what scares me the most is thinking that I wasn't the only one, that he probably didn't stop his victimizing with me.

I looked to my immediate family for guidance and support. I looked to my older brother who lived with us. His girlfriend came around a lot so I got to know her pretty well. She was four years older than I was, but, since she spent a lot of time in our apartment and we were often alone together, we had long, intimate talks. I found out that I had it pretty good compared to her. Her life was tragic. She had grown up in a foster home, too, but she had never known her family. She went from home to home, got involved with the wrong crowd; now she was with my brother. Unfortunately, they used crack cocaine, and she couldn't seem to stay away from it. One day she was found lying dead in the street from an overdose—she was just lying there with a Newport in her hand, dead. She died with no family, no money, no funeral—just a cigarette. I never got to say good-bye; she was gone, forever.

Four months later my brother came into my room and asked me for twenty dollars. Money was scarce, but he said he needed it. He came back home a little while later with two rocks of crack cocaine. I was incensed; I argued with him and tried to reason with him. I said, "You are the oldest one in our family, you are supposed to be an example for us!" He left the apartment and I felt empty and alone. There was no sound of a drum left in me; I could only hear myself sobbing as I cried all night long. My brother returned the next day; I never looked to him for support again.

Sometimes all I had were the memories of my grandmother's stories. She said that when my people migrated to Chicago they didn't have an easy life. The lives of our people had been torn apart by so many forces. Generations had been dislodged, separated from their families, sold, and treated like animals. They had lost their connection with the past—their culture, their values, their teaching stories, their religion, and their sense of family. Some retained their connection with their history; many retained only a hint of the past; a few seemed to lose it altogether.

"Freedom" dumped us into economic poverty and did not restore our culture. We tried the "white man's way" but were constantly reminded of our status by dehumanizing signs reading "whites only" and by access to only low-class jobs. Some broke through this ceiling of inequity; many did not. These bruises of cultural pounding are present in many of the social issues that our people face today.

A few days later, I was with my cousin and her little boy. We were driving down the street and she pulled over to the curb where some men were standing. She called over to the men that she wanted to make a "buy." Then she got out of the car and went into an abandoned building with them; she returned with some *coke* and sniffed it right in the car. I turned her two-year old's head so he wouldn't see what his mommie was doing. I just sat there shocked, holding him tightly, as if I could protect him from the life he was about to lead. My cousin turned to me and said sheepishly, "I'm sorry, I just have to do this."

That was it for me. That was the point I realized how crazy my life was with people dying and using drugs. My cousin was gone; my brother was gone; his girlfriend was gone. I didn't want want to end up like everyone else. I wanted to make it in my life; I wanted to pass the sound of the distant drum on to a child of my own some day. *I wanted to survive!*

Fortunately, I had someone to turn to. Mrs. Kaje-Weng, my former teacher in California, had seen something in me that few people took the time to see. In fact, she helped me to value the distant sound that I felt inside myself. When I left the fourth grade, she never lost touch with me. She wrote cards and letters to me; she paid for a summer biology class; she sent me family pictures and told me that she always thought about me; she included me in her family. She often phoned me, even when I was living with the foster families.

She called during this crisis period. I was fifteen and time was running out. I told her how depressing things were; she heard my plea for help. Then things started happening fast. She called her daughter and son-in-law, who had no children of their own. They were willing to fly me to their home in California during spring break to see if it might be possible for me to live with them. I jumped at the chance.

To say that my trip to California was a piece of heaven wouldn't be saying enough. My hostess and host, Kirsti and Gordon, took me to all the sights, fed me great meals, talked to me for hours, and even let me stay in my own bedroom! The week flew; it was like a fairy tale. At the end of the week we stood at the airport gate and said our "good-byes." Then they asked me if I would like to move to California and live with them. It was a perfect end to a perfect week, but I already knew my answer. I just couldn't leave my ten-year-old twin brothers alone in Chicago. My brothers needed me more than I needed out. I thanked this wonderful California couple and got on the plane and headed back to Chicago.

Kirsti and Gordon must have talked long and hard about my coming back because they called me a few weeks later and wondered if my brothers and I would spend some time with them while they were in Chicago for a summer conference. They came in July; shortly thereafter, they bought one-way tickets for all three of us—my twin brothers and me—to move to California. My life was turning around and the drumbeat was beginning to return.

My new home proved to be more hospitable than I had ever expected. My brothers adapted quickly to their new family, made lots of friends at school, and proceeded to eat our new parents out of house and home. I knew how much I had to be thankful for. Now I lived in a nice house, had two loving new parents, and had been accepted in a very different culture. School was different, especially being in school with a lot of white kids—we had only one white kid in our school in Chicago. I had a chance to experience very different things. I had adapted to change before, so I knew I could do it again. I had to—I didn't want my brothers, Eric and Derrick, to go through what I had gone through while I was growing up.

That first year was busy and exciting. People were really friendly to me. I enjoyed being able to move smoothly from one social group to another. I made it into cheerleading (all of the other cheerleaders were white), helped launch a girls' *stepper* group (they were mostly African-American), and just generally hung out with the rest of the student body (a real mix of ethnicity). The Steppers had the beat though; we became a hit at the assemblies, got invited to perform at other schools, and inspired similar groups wherever we performed.

I guess most people would have been content just to live the "good life" for the rest of high school, but I liked having new challenges. I liked being the first to try new things, so I sat up and listened when a group of students came into my English class to make a presentation one day toward the end of my first school year in California. I was about to make another change.

I liked school and I liked my classmates and my teachers; my life was full and I should have been content with the way things were. But, somehow this group visiting our classroom caught my attention. They seemed so supportive of each other. They seemed to know each other in a way, unlike any that I had seen before in school. They talked about trusting and caring, building community, taking responsibility for themselves, creating their own education, educating the whole person, hands-on learning, building a collective vision. Many of the terms were new to me, but I felt I wanted the sincerity and connectedness these students had in my own life.

They invited those of us who were interested in enrolling in their program for the coming year to join them in a game—a three-day simulation of society—to be conducted at Venture Lodge, an old rustic cabin located between the Santa Cruz Mountains and the Pacific Ocean. I jumped at the opportunity. Two weeks later I was riding in a bus with a bunch of strangers, singing and laughing and making ready for a whole new adventure.

We had a great time. We all slept in a big cabin, cooked meals together, played games outside, swam, and participated in a simulation of society that was run by the students and their teacher. It was also challenging; I realized that besides getting to know some other students very well, I was being challenged to think.

The final evening, all of us assembled in the big living room of the lodge—twenty-four participants, eight second-year student-coordinators, and our teacher, Gary. Then I saw something I didn't expect. At one end of the room were drums, real drums, a big conga, African drums with goat hide, tambourines, even a flute, sticks, and bells. We were making ready to participate in a creative dance. The lights were replaced by candlelight, and we became silent. The student-coordinators and our teacher started to play, and led us through some wonderful group and individual dance creations. I felt as if I was being transformed to a time when life was connected and harmonious.

For the next two hours our little group was transfixed by the movements, the flickering light, the shadows on the ceilings, the creative dance, the sounds of the instruments, and, most of all, the underlying beat of the drums. *It took me back to my roots and drew me forward to my purpose.* We seemed to move as one, and we were all directing the movement. I had never experienced anything quite like this before.

> *My grandmother told me that I have a mixed heritage. In addition to my African roots, I am also a descendant of the people of the proud Cherokee Nation. They were a nation of American Indians who lost their homeland and way of life to the onslaught of European squatters who believed it was their*

God-given destiny to radically alter the landscape and people of North America. The Cherokee also had a spirituality that inspired them to action, that defined their way of life. They, too, could hear an ancient drum. Many of them lost touch with their culture as their way of life was replaced by the "civilized" way of the white man.

The next day as we were returning home, I knew that the sound of the drum was with me. It was contained in my every heartbeat—strong, rhythmic, and steady. I knew that I had made my choice for the next school year; I would join this group.

Four months later, a new school year began. Twenty of us new students joined six second-year students to help create our version of The Learning Community. In the first three weeks of school we spent four hours each day getting to know each other, engaging in bonding exercises, and exploring ways to take charge of our education. We started to brainstorm ideas and resources for independent study; we wrote personal contracts, clarified our personal and academic goals, and developed specific content for carrying out our goals. Then we began to look for books, hands-on projects, names of potential speakers, and places where we could take field trips.

In addition to spending time deciding what we wanted to study for the year, we also spent a lot of time discussing how important it was for us to make some basic agreements to ensure that we functioned as an effective group. We talked about contracts, about giving our word, about trust and integrity. We made agreements with each other about simple, obvious things like coming to school every day, being on time, and giving full attention to whoever is speaking—norms of behavior that many high school students never follow. We gave our word to agreements; I wondered if I could keep them. Would I be able to take full initiative in the group or be fully honest with myself and others? We also agreed not to use drugs and liquor during or within a day of all class activities. We even agreed to remind each other if we were breaking our commitments. We talked about taking charge of our lives, making conscious choice, and valuing commitment, self-respect, and personal dignity.

After the first three weeks of the new school year, we returned to the old lodge in the mountains to engage in a three-day orientation to help us get ready for our school year. We wanted a focused period of time away from the distractions of home and school, so that we could create a cohesive group. In one of our more compelling experiences, we introduced ourselves to the group by telling our life stories and explaining how our life experiences had made us who we are today.

Jeremy told of his childhood trips to the Sierra Nevada Mountains with his family, playing in streams and hiking with his dad. He recalled sitting in his elementary-school desk watching the fall colors, the winter rain, and the spring blossoms around the school. He daydreamed of hiking to the top of the far mountain, building tree forts, and floating down streams in inner-tubes. He didn't like school; it cooped him up too much. He joined our program to find a way to become more motivated and more interested in school. I saw him as a "country boy." Until now, I had never been around someone who spent time in nature. I thought he was different but he was easy to be around, always making funny jokes out of awkward situations.

Greg shared how he had always been in gifted classes and got good grades in school. He shared a variety of his interests—he was a long distance-runner and liked to act. He talked about how he "lost it" and went into a depression. He said his ability to act had helped him pretend in life but that he lost the ability to pretend, and that now it was just too difficult for him to deal with life. He said the doctor had prescribed *Prozac* to help him hide the feeling that he could no longer "pretend" away. He joined our group because he thought we would just let him be and he needed to figure out what to make of life. He seemed distant at times, but he had the capacity to be honest about his life. I was touched by his vulnerability.

Shawn was a big, tough-looking, white guy. He said he grew up in Army towns because his mom was in the service. I had never stopped to consider that women in the Army had time to have kids, I wondered what it was like for her. Shawn spoke of having lived in the tough parts of town where he was a minority, having to be tough to keep from being run over by people, and always moving away before he made any friends. He described himself as an average student who wanted to make a few close friends. I identified with his courage, but I had a hard time getting close to him.

I liked Jenny right away. She and her sister, Wendy, were both in the group. They were warm and friendly with no pretenses. They had come to this country from El Salvador; both were dark-skinned and had features like their Mayan ancestors. I felt an easy kinship with both of them. Jenny told a story about how her family had traveled nearly three-thousand miles through Guatemala and Mexico to escape the brutal civil war in her country. She was a survivor, like me. I liked her even more when she said, with tears coming down her cheeks, that she was a good student and was in our program because she wanted to make something of herself. I intended to be her friend. Wendy was open and empathetic; I knew that we would become good friends, too.

Kristie, the nature lover, spoke of how a butterfly landed on her nose when she was five, how she had always loved nature, especially birds, and was an amateur taxidermist. She said she came into the program because she wanted to help protect the environment. She knew she could build her studies around real issues and take action to stop the abuse of the earth. She talked of how she and a friend liked to go to Santa Cruz and sit for hours talking to homeless people about their lives. I could feel her sensitivity and felt I could trust her.

Angel, the other African-American student, was a standout singer. Like me, she hadn't had a father in her life, but unlike me, she had had a strong mother. Angel was a devout Christian and very strong in her beliefs. She was an interesting blend of the hip culture—she dressed cool, had her hair braided, could "talk the talk" (although she didn't have a foul mouth), and was a great stepper. We had known each other before joining the program, even though she was much younger than I. She wanted to be in the program because she felt she would be accepted as a full human being, not just a gifted singer. She didn't want to be just another "number" in a classroom or someone regarded as lazy or having an attitude because she missed classes or was late. She wanted to help make school become exciting so that she would be inspired to be there all the time. Angel already seemed to have a steady beat of the drum inside her.

Janna was a tall, introspective young woman with long brown curly hair. She talked of having attended private schools. Her mother had taken her sister out of school to be educated at home. Janna never watched television and she read a lot. She had been enrolled in honors classes in public school and got good grades. She joined us, she said, because she wanted to work closely with other committed people in creating a better world. She really seemed to believe in what she said.

Adrienne always shared well-stated, yet understated, solutions during our community-building activities. Most of our early activities were pretty boisterous, so her points were often ignored; but she had a way of persisting without pushing so that, when the most assertive members got tired of shouting, her point of view often stood out as the most sensible. Like Kristie, she had actually moved into the district to be in our program. Adrienne, who had been an honor student at her other school, longed for the personal emphasis of our program and wanted to have more freedom to design her studies. She really wanted to be part of the world—not to just study about it.

We had such a cross-section of humanity assembled in our group! We had sophomores, juniors, and seniors; we had excellent students and students wanting to find their excellence; we had students who had been born in Mexico, Guatemala, El Salvador, the Philippines, and the United States. We had a range of students, some from solid, loving families and some from non-existent or dysfunctional families. Each, regardless of privilege, had his or her personal scars, some deeper than others; each had his or her own personal strengths as well. We all shared a need for a fuller life. Also, we shared a common desire to make our own lives better and to make the world better.

I told my story about growing up in Chicago. Many of the things I had never told a soul before. I cried, almost uncontrollably, when I told about the rape; it was the first time that I had confided in anyone since that cold, winter day in Chicago. Wendy came over and comforted me. Several other students gathered around the pillow on which I was sitting and held me while I sobbed. Other students just sat in place and cried with me. I felt safe and I felt loved. I had never felt so accepted by so many people at one time.

As I sat there, surrounded by my new brothers and sisters, I could hear the strong beating of my heart punctuated by the quiet sounds of weeping in the room. More than that, I could feel another beat emerging in the room, it was the beginning of a beat that was new to me. It sounded as if its source was that of many drums. It was a hint of what was to come, the beat of the group's collective drum. These people were becoming part of my family, and I was joining theirs. I felt at home. I could hear and I could feel a strong beat inside and around my heart.

Passage Two:
Co-creating a Vision

Following the River to the Sea

Jeremy

I have always been intrigued by rivers. When I was a young boy, my dad took me to the high Sierras. We always camped in the high meadows near little streams. He left me alone for hours while I played out my heroic fantasies in and around the water. One time I was a trapper being chased by a ferocious band of Indians. Another time I leapt Tarzan-like into the water, narrowly escaping a group of native head-hunters. My favorite role was that of an army private sneaking through the jungles of the Pacific being pursued by the enemy.

My characters came out of a string of action movies that I watched as a young boy. The imagined places changed; the faces of the enemy changed; but I was always the hero; and, somehow, I always found a way to be a hero or to save a beautiful woman from evil.

Sometimes I would build a little wooden raft out of sticks, usually no bigger than the palm of my hand. I would let it float along a quiet pool until it got to the faster part of the stream. Suddenly, it would surge down the rapids. I was close behind, chasing it as fast as I could go, jumping back and forth across the tiny creek and scampering over slippery rocks. All the while I imagined a great adventure unfolding—complete with arrows or spears or bullets flying in the air. I would save the beautiful maiden with one hand and steer the boat around rocks and snags with the other.

When the family outing was over, we went back to the San Francisco Peninsula where we lived. I watched the little stream from the window of the car and continued my fantasies in my mind's eye as the car sped along on its journey. Sometimes I closed my eyes and imagined or dozed off into a dream. When my eyes opened, I would be surprised to see that the little stream had given way to a bigger and faster one. As we traveled down the mountain, the stream had been joined by so many other streams and become so large that my boyish fantasies dissolved—I was too young to see myself in such turbulence. Instead, I just sat mesmerized by the ever-increasing power of the river. By the time we got close to home, some four hours later, I had alternated through several catnaps, hero-fantasies, and intriguing thoughts about rivers. As we crossed the San Francisco-Oakland Bay Bridge on the last leg home, I remember having two questions: "I wonder if any of my little rafts ever floated this far?" and "Where does all the water go when it reaches the ocean?"

I've always been one to try to figure things out. Perhaps it was my inquisitive nature to look for patterns in things, or maybe I was influenced by a little game my grandmother used to play with me. She always pretended that things needed fixing around the house. A lot of her appliances weren't too modern, so I was able to open them with just a screwdriver. She would say, "Jeremy, my toaster isn't working. Will you fix it for me?"

I always took the bait. We went to my grampa's toolbox and armed ourselves with a screwdriver, a pair of pliers, and some electrician's tape. Then off we went to repair whatever didn't work. We took the bottom off the toaster or took the plug apart and looked at everything. Then my grandmother asked me, "What do you think is going on in here, Jeremy?"

Sometimes I thought about how little rivers come together to form larger rivers. Then I made up some explanation about the little wires and coils in the toaster. I am sure that I seldom made any sense, but grandmas are very forgiving. When she thought that I had gone on long enough about the inner workings of the toaster, she nodded her head as if she understood and asked, "Well, do you think you've got it fixed yet?"

By this time, I was eager to see if it worked, so I put the old toaster back together again, and we plugged it in. "Wow," I said as it started heating up, "Look grandma. It works!" Then, off we went to fix the sewing machine, the vacuum cleaner, or one of her standing lamps—I "fixed" them all.

When I started in school, I was a pretty curious, active, and energetic guy. All the other kids and all the little attractions that lined the classroom were big invitations to me to get involved. Of course, I soon learned that I was allowed to touch only what the teacher wanted me to touch and play only when the teacher wanted me to play. I was confused by all the limitations placed on me, but eager to figure out how I get my hands on everything.

Schools had rules. Some of the rules made sense: wait your turn, don't grab someone else's belongings, don't hurt people. Some of the rules didn't make sense: stay inside, sit down and be quiet, and don't tease the girls. Some of the rules just didn't take: keep your seat, leave things alone, and quit talking to your friends. I was constantly in trouble. In the fourth grade, I probably spent more time in the hall than in the classroom. I didn't do anything really bad; I just wanted to be free to climb and run and scream and interact freely with everyone.

By junior high, I had school pretty well figured out. I was supposed to be receptive to what the teacher had planned; I was to remain quiet, and respond when I was asked to. The teacher, in turn, decided when we were ready to learn and what we would learn. She made the decisions, and told me when I could get involved. And if I didn't play along, my parents or the principal got involved. I didn't like it; I still longed to be outside; I wanted to hike in the mountains, play in the rivers, and climb trees. I compensated for my inactivity by being the class clown.

I spent many sessions in the principal's office. My parent conferences always were the same: "Jeremy, why can't you be a good student like your sister?" "Jeremy, you are very smart. Why don't you apply yourself?" "Jeremy, you should hang out with better kids." "Jeremy, why can't you behave yourself?"

My teachers didn't like it when I acted out or when I talked to my friends during class. They hated it when I was a wise guy. I had developed a pretty annoying, sarcastic tone. When I attempted to "go away" and take sanctuary in my daydreams, they didn't like that either. I could be floating down some rapids, making ready to save someone.

Suddenly, I would become aware that the teacher had asked me one of those "Caught ya!" questions. I didn't have the slightest idea what she had just asked me. Sometimes, I could faintly recall the echo of her last few words and I scrambled to say something that sounded like it might fit with those words. Sometimes, it worked; more often, it didn't.

One time in high school, when the teacher invited my parents to come for a conference, they tried to go "clinical" on me. My parents and counselor thought that maybe something was wrong with me. They sent me to a psychiatrist who prescribed medicine for Attention Deficit Disorder. I took the medicine for two days and got so jumpy that I quit taking it. My mom thought that it must have "kicked in" the third or fourth day, because I had calmed down quite a bit.

It was no puzzle to me what the problem was. I was bored and tired of being controlled. I wanted to be actively involved with things. School didn't offer me anything that was mine. The teacher made the assignments; I was supposed to do what I was told. The classes seemed so predictable—listen to a lecture, read an assignment, answer questions, take a test. If this was the school's way of preparing me for life, it was pretty unrealistic. I hadn't seen any examples of life, in my short life, that looked like school.

Some of the books and stories that I had to read didn't interest me in the least. I felt like life for my teachers must be pretty boring or bland. Yet they tried to force me to read their assignments. When I didn't read them, they told my parents, "Jeremy just isn't a reader." I didn't doubt that the statement was true. I didn't read, at least anything that was assigned. I certainly didn't count the war and adventure stories that I read late into the night as "reading." I actually considered my interest in these stories simply a bad habit which I carefully hid from my parents.

As my high school experience progressed, I figured out that the price was too high for me to continue to be physically provocative in the classroom. I settled for making annoying comments, taking verbal potshots, and assuming a cynical attitude. Unfortunately, my bad attitude spread to all my classes, even band. I loved to play my clarinet. I was pretty good at it. But after the band teacher tired of my remarks and had me leave class, I decided to quit the class and quit playing my instrument. My mom and stepfather were so angry that they threatened to send me to a private high school. I looked for other options. I didn't want to go away to school and leave all my friends.

I was just completing my junior year. One of my senior friends had been in an interdisciplinary studies program at the other high school in our district. However, he always seemed so serious about what his class was doing, which made me pretty skeptical. I figured that if you liked school, something must be wrong with you. But, with the threat of being carted away to a private school, I thought that I had better find a place that worked for me. So I went with my friend to one of the open houses held by The Learning Community.

My parents went to the meeting with me. The teacher, Gary, explained the program:

> *Our group meets for four hours per day, five days a week for the full school year. We start our year by considering two fundamental questions: "Who am I?" and "What do I wish to learn?" The quest to answer both questions leads us to a study of the whole person. We learn who we are by investigating our physical, emotional, intellectual, social, ecological, and spiritual dimensions. The twenty-five students who are accepted each year enter our program committed to pursue personal meaning and personal development in each of these areas.*
>
> *My primary purpose is to join in this search, while helping the group to strike a balance in their studies.*

I'll have to admit that I didn't really understand what he was talking about; maybe it was because I wasn't listening. I spent my time looking around the room to see if I could find signs of life. The students who spoke talked about supporting one another and valuing the friendships they had made. That was a good sign. So I started paying more attention as Gary continued:

> *The Learning Community is a place where you can co-create your studies with a community consisting of your fellow students and me, your teacher. We all share the responsibility for developing the group's curriculum. Each of us has an important role in creating the program.*

> *The student is asked to think about what he or she really wants out of life and school—personally, interpersonally, academically, and vocationally. Then he or she is asked to create a study contract that reflects these purposes.*

> *Each new group of students recreates the program each year. I will lead your group through a process in which you can develop a set of common goals. Your group goals will form the basis for the group experience that we will share throughout the year.*

As Gary spoke, I started thinking about things that I would like to do if I were in the program. My thoughts were of adventure—hands-on or literary. I wondered if this group would really support my doing exactly what I wanted to do. I wasn't convinced that they would like the things that I liked. Also, I was interested to hear what the teacher's role was in the group experience. I listened as he answered my unspoken question:

> *In addition to the individual student input and the group's planned activities, I help the group become autonomous. Also, I teach a Psychological Systems seminar and develop some thematic units related to events in the world.*

I watched and listened. This approach was foreign to me. I needed time to figure out what this theory meant in a real experience. And, most importantly, I would be on the lookout to see whether this was just a smoke screen for the same old school experience.

First, I had to get in the program. My real dad lived in New York City. He moved there after he and my mom got divorced, while I was in the fifth grade. I didn't like thinking about the divorce, because it also meant my divorce from family trips to the Sierras. My dad never lost touch with me, though. We talked, long distance, at least twice each week.

I called and told him that I was thinking about applying to the program. He was worried about me. He wanted me to get into a good university and he wanted me to be with the right kind of kids. I couldn't really answer all his questions about the program. I did tell him that it sounded like something I wanted to do and that I had to submit an application in one week. My dad called the school and talked to Gary the next day. My dad wanted to visit the class, meet the teacher, and figure out what was best for me. He flew out to California five days later.

My dad must have liked what he saw in the class because he got real excited about the program. He made a strong plea on my behalf with the teacher. He even called the teacher when he returned to New York to tell him about how we engaged in frequent intellectual discussions over the phone. We had discussed several college-level books, including *Candide*. Maybe his call helped; one week later, I was accepted into the program.

My senior year started with great expectations. I was really starting over. I didn't know these people, and they didn't know me. My reputation hadn't followed me over, so I was safe for now just being me. I felt strange, though. I found myself in a highly racially mixed group; I wasn't used to this. My elementary and middle schools were in nearly all-white neighborhoods, and our schools were basically white, with a few Asians.

I looked around the Learning Community classroom. I was struck by the diversity—Caucasian, African-American, Latino, and Asian. Some of our students were born in other countries—the Philippines, Guatemala, Mexico, El Salvador, and India. As I got to know everybody, it turned out that three kids whom I thought were like me, were not. One was part American Indian, another who called himself Mestizo (or mixed blood), was from Cuba, and another was from Chile. I felt like I was attending an international school. It took some getting used to for me. Also, I didn't know if I could get along with some of the outspoken girls in the class.

As we got to know each other, many of these differences vanished. I found myself connecting to people, and I forgot about their ethnicity or gender. We were all trying to understand the opportunity that we had before us, and that required that we put our differences aside. I tried to apply my usual thinking skills to the task of figuring things out. I wanted things to work out for me, but I didn't want to get trapped into doing things that I didn't want to do. I wondered how we were ever going to agree on things with so many different people with so many diverse ideas.

One of our commitments was to come to school every day and to be on time. Some of our students had admitted to having a lax attitude about attendance; they were concerned about the consequences if they broke their commitment. It didn't take very long to find out what would happen. The next day Tamika was late and we waited to see what Gary would do.

When Tamika came in, we were setting up our agenda for the day. Gary interrupted the planning discussion and said, "Tamika, I'd like to share a strategy that all of us can use to give us more power in our lives. Would you like to help me out?"

"No problem," she said, in a matter-of-fact way. It always surprised me how rationally she responded to Gary and some of the other students in our program. Anytime I criticized her or disagreed with her, she'd get pretty hostile with me. I didn't stop to think how I may have provoked her.

Gary engaged Tamika, not in an authoritarian way, but in the way that a friend might offer suggestions: "When you entered our program, you said that you wanted to understand yourself better and that you wanted to improve yourself. Those are major commitments that you've made to yourself. To get to that place, you may wish to take a closer look at what you are creating. Then you could ensure that your *your actions* would be consistent with *your words*."

Janna spoke up: "It's been tough for me to get to school on time most of my life. It's been even tougher trying to change my old habit patterns; my old habits are pretty strong. I'm starting to realize that taking control of my life doesn't mean that I do whatever I want to—it means that I do whatever I agree to do. When my actions don't match my words, I feel a conflict inside of me. At times, when I haven't come through for a friend, it has cost me respect from a person I valued. Worse yet, at times, when I haven't come through for myself, I've stopped trusting myself."

"Tamika, would you like to go back over the events of the morning to see how things may have gotten out of control?" Gary asked.

She knew that Gary wasn't trying to be preachy. Yet, her response was honest and direct: "Sure, but you've got to know that I'm not a morning person; and I'm definitely not going to come to school with my hair looking bad!" I doubted that Gary was going to change anything with words.

"Good, Tamika, you know what you want. What's left is figuring out how to get it. Maybe we could explore how to get everything that you want," Gary offered.

"Sure, but I don't see what else I could have done; I already said I am not coming to school looking like I just crawled out of bed," was Tamika's response.

Gary went on; he didn't seem preachy, but he seldom let up in this kind of situation. The good news was that Tamika didn't react as if she were being admonished: "Think about it as if you are on a path, your path. You want three things—to be in control, to keep your word, and to look presentable at school. But you end up getting only one thing—you look presentable. It's too late to get number one or two this time, but there is a way to get it next time."

Tamika seemed genuinely curious: "How can I do that? I'm willing, but I'll have to warn you: I've never been on time to things in my life."

"The solution lies in sifting through the current circumstance. Think back through this morning and see if you can figure at which point you chose to be late," he said.

"I what? I didn't choose to be late!" Tamika countered.

"Then who is in charge in your life?" Gary asked.

"I am!" Tamika said, as if to put her verbal foot down.

"OK. If you are really in charge, then you are accountable for all that results—good or bad— from your actions," he said, "So, let's get back to finding your *choice point*."

"My what?" Tamika was getting a little frustrated. I think she was afraid that, the way this was going, she might have to change her behavior. She didn't really seem to want to do that.

Gary replied: "Your *choice point*, Tamika. If you're in charge of yourself, or want to be, then you are in charge of all the micro-moments of your life. If you can find the moment that you chose to be late and can be aware of that moment, the next time you have the opportunity, you can get control of that moment." He just laid the idea out and waited for her to respond.

"Now wait a minute. Are you saying that I *chose* to be late?" Tamika looked quizzical. "Why would I do that?"

"That question is for you, not me." Gary responded. "I'm sure that some-where in your morning you lost control of the situation, and that you were no longer in charge of the outcome. At what point did that happen?"

"Well, if I had gotten up when my alarm rang, I could've fixed my hair and got to school on time," she replied. Her voice slowed as if she was seeing herself in some kind of slow-motion, instant-replay video. "But, I have such a hard time getting up in the morning," she said in a pleading voice.

"What time do you usually go to bed?" asked Joanna.

"Pretty late, I like to stay up and talk on the phone or read," she answered.

"It looks like you've got a lot of information to apply here, Tamika. Perhaps you'll want to watch your behaviors over the next few days. You've got an opportunity to take charge here," Gary said. He seemed content to leave Tamika to solve her own dilemma and move on.

Then he turned to the class and said, "We can all apply this kind of thought process to our lives. We can take control of our lives. We can help each other, too. I certainly don't want to be the enforcer here. It's much more effective when people take responsibility for themselves. Why don't we each take charge and help make this a strong group? All we need to do is remind people to be aware and to account for themselves. If our group members are willing to take charge, our reminders become their gifts, not criticisms."

Over the next few days, everyone's attendance improved. Either the technique of watching for our personal choice points worked, or the prospect of spending several minutes every day being confronted by our peers worked. Whatever the case, we needed to brainstorm ideas and make ready for developing our studies. I was eager to see just how all these people's ideas were going to get worked in. I wondered what kind of sense we could make out of it.

I had been working on my study contract since the first day of school. I wanted to have fun this year, and I wanted to follow my interests. I knew that I could complete my graduation requirements, but I had other goals that would be harder to accomplish. I wanted to go to the University of California, and I wondered how I could strike a balance between my interests and college prerequisites. I needed to find a way to hike in the mountains, experiment with my music, and read what I wanted—although I figured that I had read all the good war stories— while developing skills that would prepare me for my life.

In addition to being together as a class for twenty-hours a week, each of us met with Gary for thirty minutes every other week. This way, he could develop a closeness to us and to our studies. We could get his input into our studies, develop a better personal relationship with him, and actually teach him what we were learning. He and I always approached my work and the evaluation of my work from a common place—as if we were doing it together. I didn't feel judged; I felt supported. We usually agreed on my grades, although sometimes, when I was being strongly self-critical, he urged me to be "lighten up on yourself." Once in a while, when I was trying to slide by, he urged me not to "delude yourself." Gary encouraged me to set my own standards and to do my work to please myself.

In one of my biweekly conferences with Gary, I told him that I was having trouble completing my English contract. I was setting up a reading list. It was easy to pick a few books off the school's official reading list, but I couldn't figure what to add that represented my interests. Gary asked me if there was any book that I had wanted to read, but hadn't found the time to read. Some of my friends had long lists of books that they didn't have time to read; that wasn't my problem. I told Gary that my dad and I had read and discussed major classics, but that I really liked war novels. Gary said, "Well, why don't you select one or two war novels?"

"I've already read all the good ones," I said.

He got up and invited me to look over our small classroom library. I doubted that this little library would have anything that I hadn't read or would be interested in reading. Gary reached up and pulled out a worn, yellowed paper-back novel. The picture on the front looked like a war scene. The book was *Battle Cry* by Leon Uris. I started reading it that night and couldn't put it down. It was like a dream; I was in ecstasy. I was completing my homework and enjoying it. I went to Gary and asked for another suggestion. He asked me if I had read *The Naked and the Dead* by Norman Mailer. I wasn't sure where he was getting these books; I thought that I had read every war novel that was ever written. Here were two that I hadn't even heard of, and they both were compelling. When I read them, I identified with the main characters. They helped me get in fantasy what I couldn't get in reality—drama, suspense, action. There was also an underlying sense of justice that the character helped to bring into the world.

Our students got their individual contracts in order. Each of us created course descriptions in five curricular areas—physical development, psychology, communication process, human ecology, and environmental studies. We varied our course titles to fit our needs or grade levels. Since the group was of mixed grade-level and we each had different graduation requirements, we got credit in different courses even though we shared the same experience each day. Our program was probably structured more like the old one-room school house.

I was curious to see how the program would come together. In some ways, I felt as if I was still the little boy in my grandmother's house trying to figure out the internal working of the toaster. I had ideas and I could ramble on about them, but I really didn't have a clue how this experience was going to be tied together.

As part of our contract development and in preparation for our group studies, Gary had us bring in all our ideas to share. We brainstormed activities in each area of study—physical, emotional, intellectual, societal, and environmental. We rolled out big sheets of butcher paper and recorded our ideas as the class shared them. We ended up creating "mind-maps," ways of organizing data that looked like big nerve cells and fibers. We spent five exciting sessions just exploring ideas in the subject areas. With each student sharing his or her idea on each subject area, we ended up with literally hundreds of ideas. It gave us an idea of just how rich the world of ideas is. When we had finished, I became excited at the prospect of pursuing some of the issues that the students had shared.

When we came into The Learning Community, many of us didn't know what to expect. It was the first time that most of us had been in a learning environment in which we were responsible for the content. We had a three-week calendar on our wall; it was blank when we came into the classroom the first day. Some of us wondered aloud how we could create enough learning activities to fill it for four hours per day, five days a week for a whole year. After our brainstorming session, some of us began to wonder if we would have enough time in the school year to do all the things that we wanted to do.

After we finished our individual contracts and started our studies, we were ready to plan our daily calendar. Gary cautioned us that if we simply filled our calendar with events, we would lose focus. He said that we needed to work toward some kind of group purpose to bring meaning to our work. He offered to facilitate a process to help us develop our group goals.

Gary got out the butcher paper again and tacked it to the wall. He laid out pieces of colored paper, felt pens, and index cards. We gathered around him in a semicircle against one of the walls in our classroom. He asked us to close our eyes and follow along as he spoke.

> *Imagine that you are sitting in class on the last day of school. You are very satisfied with the year that you have just created together. You start to talk to each other about the activities you have shared—field trips, speakers, discussions, debates, projects, trips, service projects, and the like. As you look back over the year, note which five or six things stand out as having made this the best year that you have ever had in school. What specific activities stand out for you?*

When we opened our eyes, Gary asked us to write five of our best ideas on index cards. Many of these ideas had been making their way into our conversations, our contracts, and our brainstorms in the three weeks since school had started. After we finished compiling our lists, Gary asked us to pare down our lists to our three most important ideas. That was the hard part.

Each of us had our favorite ideas. I wanted to organize a backpacking trip for the class and go somewhere that I'd never gone before—I wasn't sure where—as long as it was far away and in the mountains. I wanted us to create a talent show in which we could share our acting or musical talents. I wanted us to have some speakers that would talk about the effects of smoking and how to quit—I didn't think that I'd ever say anything like that in public, but I had secretly wanted to stop smoking for a long time.

Tamika wanted to invite a civil-rights attorney to speak to our class. She wanted to set up a mock trial in which she would assign courtroom roles for us to act out. And she wanted to teach us some stepping routines that we could perform to music.

Greg wanted us to write and stage a play. He wanted the class to read *Slaughterhouse Five* by Kurt Vonnegut, then discuss the morality of war. He wanted us to investigate the role that media play in shaping people's opinions. Also he wanted us to watch the videotape, *Manufacturing Consent,* featuring Noam Chomsky.

Shawn wanted us to play Ultimate Frisbee, an airborne soccer game. He wanted us to participate in a ropes course to help us confront our fears and learn how to work better as a team. Plus he wanted us to have a music jam, in which each student would create sounds on improvised instruments.

Jenny wanted us to investigate the politics and cultures of Latin America. As part of the study, she could share her experiences in El Salvador, and we could read Mayan folk tales and watch *El Norte.* She also wanted us to set aside days in which we could do art projects or create a mural together.

Kristie wanted to make a presentation on birds, wildlife rescue, and bring in a live falcon. She wanted us to participate in a creek clean-up project. She also wanted us to learn about the ecology of San Francisco Bay.

Janna wanted us to discuss creative approaches to education. She wanted us to work with children. She was especially passionate about discussing gender and body issues and getting a speaker from a battered women's shelter.

Angel wanted us to earn money to support an overseas development project in Ghana and get overseas pen pals. She wanted us to listen to her gospel choir. She suggested that we read and discuss *Sula* by Toni Morrison. I was surprised when she said she wanted us to go to the beach and study tide pools. I didn't know that she had outdoor interests, too.

Adrienne wanted us follow the results of the Overpopulation Conference in Cairo. She wanted us to study organic gardening and plant a group garden. She suggested that we explore vegetarianism.

Gary offered to conduct weekly seminars in which we could investigate models of psychology and spirituality. He wanted to facilitate a weekly support group. He also offered to help us focus on major social and environmental issues that are surfacing in the world.

The more ideas that were shared, the more our group got excited. Joe wanted to go to southern California to Joshua Tree National Wildlife Sanctuary, and he wanted to play the sitar for us. Joanna, whose father was a publisher, wanted to introduce us to publishing. Alma, who was born in Guatemala, wanted us to come to her house and have her mother teach us how to make tamales. Erika wanted us to study the election propositions that were on the ballot in the coming election. Each student shared three exciting ideas. It was unbelievable, I had one of my most exciting days in school and all we did was talk! Still, I didn't know how we were going to pull this off. The ideas were exciting enough on their own, but I doubted that we could create a focus.

As each student presented his or her ideas, Gary asked us to watch for patterns or relationships to emerge. We wrote our ideas in big bold letters on pieces of paper and grouped those that seemed related. As our ideas were shared, I actually began to see some patterns starting to form.

Gary challenged our group to develop a descriptive phrase for each group of events. He insisted, though, that we create the phrases as a group and get the whole class to reach consensus on the phrasing before we moved on to another group of ideas. He suggested that we imagine a student's offering as a beach ball thrown into the air. Then our challenge was to keep the idea afloat by nudging the concept along. That way, we reinforced the other person's idea while embellishing it with words of our own. The process was quite a challenge—one that led us to a greater level of cooperation.

It was quite a task to bring twenty-five people to consensus on one small phrase, but we made it a team effort. We supported each other's ideas and tried to build on ideas instead of shooting them down. The whole process of sharing, grouping, phrasing, and agreeing took hours. It was an emotional strain, but no one seemed to want to quit. When we finished our task, we had created seven categories with seventy-five activities for the first semester. And, we had done it ourselves.

Gary pointed out that the grouping of these events represented our *group objectives*. Our final groupings were:

To Expand And Express Our Creativity
Activities: *Creative Day, Invite Playwright To Speak, Work With Clay, Make and Sell Crafts, Make Dream Catchers, Write Short Stories, Watch <u>The Wave</u>, a play about fascism, Make Masks And Role Play, Write A Book, Stage A Talent Show, Have A Music Jam, Write Poetry.*

To Understand The Structure Of Society
Activities: *Read <u>Teenage Liberation Handbook</u> by Grace Llewellyn, Speaker-Civil Rights Attorney, Policeman's Perspective On Violence In America, Read <u>People's History Of United States</u>, Watch-<u>Eyes On The Prize</u> Series, Watch Documentary On Harvey Milk, Discuss Censorship, Study The Homeless, Speaker From Battered Women's Shelter, Watch <u>Manufacturing Consent</u>, Discuss How We Are Influenced By The Media, Research Subliminal Advertisement, Conduct Mock Trial, Abortion Debate, Work In Soup Kitchen, Debate Affirmative Action, Visit Courtroom In Session, Work In Political Campaigns, Watch <u>El Norte</u>, Watch <u>Cry Freedom</u>, Study Indigenous People, Study Latin American Politics, Study Women's Issues, Study Gays and Lesbians, Read <u>Slaughterhouse Five</u>, Watch <u>King Of Hearts</u>, Invite Song Writer, Go To A Shakespearean Play, Study Election Issues and Ballot Measures.*

To Experience Nature
Activities: *Hike At Jasper Ridge Biological Reserve, Visit St. Patrick's Seminary Grounds, Speaker On South American Butterflies, Go Stargazing With A*

Telescope, Study Deforestation, Backpack At Joshua Tree, Hike At The Baylands, Go Tide pooling, Study "Deep Ecology."

To Explore Our Minds, Bodies, And Spirit

Activities: Play New Games—Non-Competitive Games, Host A Yoga Teacher, Watch Bill Moyers' *Healing And The Mind*, Set Up A Writing Workshop, Check Out Book Store & Library Resources, Learn How To Stop Smoking, Speaker-Naturopathic Healer, Go On Ropes Course, Play Frisbee Soccer, Study Birth Control, Discussion And Speaker On AIDS, Discuss Gender And Body Issues, Film On Anorexia, Study Zen Buddhism And Tai Chi.

To Appreciate The Richness Of Our Diversity

Activities: Research & Present Our Families' Heritage, Mayan Fairy Tales, Read And Discuss <u>Sula</u>, Watch Swedish Film <u>My Life As A Dog</u>, Attend Concert By Samate-drummer From Africa, Watch <u>American Me</u>, Make Tamales Together, Foods From Other Cultures, Watch Folklorico Dance, Go On An Overnight Trip, Watch <u>Black To The Promised Land</u> Documentary, Write To Global Pen Pals, Attend Kwanzaa Ceremony, Listen To Gospel Choir.

To Work With Children

Activities: Participate In Environmental Volunteers Training, Organize Food Drive, Work In Children's Garden At Duveneck Ranch, Raise Money For Children's Garden In Mexicali, Work At The Ronald McDonald House.

T O Help Conserve The Environment

Activities: Plant Trees With Magic, Take Organic Gardening Classes, Plant An Organic Garden, Rain Forest Awareness, Beach Clean-up, Research Vegetarianism, Study Endangered Species, Set Up Home And Classroom Recycling, Research Electric Cars, Research Ways To Conserve At Home, Study Current Issues, Study Global Pollution / Observe Bay Area, Write Legislature Regarding Local Issues.

We breathed a collective sigh of relief when we finished our task. Each of us had contributed to the group's proposed activities for the semester, sorted them into similar categories, and agreed on seven objectives to guide our group. I could see that our group was coming together.

We weren't finished though. Gary wanted us to go the next step. He asked us to look over our group objectives and see if we could we find a relationships among the objectives. There was something about the process of finding a relationship that seemed familiar to me. I felt as if I had seen all of this before, but I wasn't sure where or when.

Everyone jumped into the act. We had written out objectives on poster board and placed them in the middle of our circle; then looked for relationships. "Hey look, *experiencing nature* and *conserving the environment* are related," noted Paki. We moved the two objective posters together. After some discussion, the group agreed with Paki. Then we looked at the remaining objectives.

"How about putting *exploring ourselves* and *expressing our creativity* together?" suggested Janna. Once again, a discussion brewed. By now, we had become pretty good at asserting ourselves in a public debate; it was interesting to see how everyone got into the act and how everyone seemed to know exactly how they wanted the objectives sequenced.

The task was completed when Wendy noted that "*Society, diversity*, and *working with children* were left, and she described how they were related." After we agreed, our ideas had come together. It was truly a group effort.

Our next task was to find a common phrase that represented our groupings of objectives. Gary told us that we had progressed from specific activities to group objectives to group goals. Our next step was to formulate our goals. After more spirited collaboration, we developed the following *Group Goals*.

Goal 1: To Enhance Our Personal Awareness
- To expand and express our creativity
- To explore our minds, bodies, and spirit

Goal 2: To Learn To Live Together As Human Beings
- To understand the structure of society
- To appreciate the richness of our diversity
- To work with children

Goal 3: To Develop A Healthy Relationship With The Planet
- To experience nature
- To help conserve the environment

As Gary described our last step, I realized why today's goal-setting activity seemed so familiar. I'd had an experience like this before; but it wasn't in school. It was in my dad's car when I was a little boy. The little streams that joined to form larger streams, the larger streams that turned into rivers. I remembered them vividly. Here we had events flowing into objectives and objectives flowing into goals. With that realization, I anticipated the next assignment. We were instructed to create an overarching statement that represented our groups vision, our large purpose. It wasn't easy. We all wanted to cling to specific elements in our objectives and our goals. After nearly an hour of discussion, our group finally broke through. We found a way to embrace everyone's higher ideals into a single vision statement:

> *We wish to build a strong, effective community so we can explore and contribute to the world.*

Our collective vision in the goal-setting process was like the ocean in my childhood experience. As an innocent child, I wondered where all the rivers went when they got to the ocean. Earlier today, I wondered where our ideas would go if we created a collective vision. I found that, like streams in a watershed, each individual's interests and values were included in each objective and in each goal. Our final *vision* embraced them all.

Passage Three:
Healing the Wounds

Finding the Face Behind the Mask

Greg

Two years ago was a blurry, vague, and surreal time in my life. I missed the second semester of school because of depression. I experienced a seizure, the world of psychiatry, and more emotions than my brain and body could handle. I needed to understand who I was. I wanted others to understand how I felt. I just couldn't break through the mask that I seemed to wear.

I was putting a great amount of pressure on myself to make "weight" for wrestling and get good grades at the same time. I ran constantly, never satisfied with my physical condition. I was addicted to exercise. I developed a form of anorexia, eating little and exercising nonstop. Running became an obligation, a duty in my mind. Finally, just as a soda can explodes from rapid shaking, my body and mind gave in to the pressure.

I was driven to action by thoughts that didn't make sense: "I have to run. Maybe I can run for two days, 48 hours. Better yet, I could run across the United States and become President!"

My mind was racing, pounding thoughts like a broken record: "Your life stinks. Get away from everything. Go in the mountains alone." I felt trapped. I wanted to run away.

I passed the time by mumbling, sitting on the couch, watching TV. "Am I ever going to get out of this?!" I was crying, not knowing why. My energy was low. I felt that I couldn't perform a simple task—like going to the store with Mom. I yelled and screamed at mom and dad, but didn't mean it. My dog lay on the floor looking at me with worried eyes.

> I'm writing right now,
> I'm not sure why or how.
> Not for an assignment,
> But to end my confinement.
> My confinement in my head.
> To write the things said,
> In my head.

I have *depression*. Many people don't know what that means, sometimes I don't either. It is not comparable to the flu or a broken leg. It grows and eats away at the life inside. I've been asked "What is depression?" by lots of people. Now I ask myself. I ask: "What happened?" "How did I feel?" "Why?" It was a hard time to live. Rather, I existed, but I didn't live.

I remember sitting on the couch. I couldn't deal with life and emotions. I watched TV and ate cookies. I gave up. It was, for me, a form of suicide. I chose not to live because it was too hard.

At first, I wanted to run away. Actually, I wanted to run away and then come back. After a run, I would come back drained of my bad thoughts and feelings. I ran and ran before I finally collapsed. If I thought I was overweight, before I went to bed, I'd set my alarm for early in the morning. At first, I set my alarm for 6:30 a.m., and I would run for half an hour before school started. Gradually, my starting time edged back closer to midnight as wrestling season progressed. I wore sweaters, two pairs of sweat pants. Once, I ran for four hours. I ran at Rancho San Antonio Park. There's a PG&E road that meanders up to a summit and then down. I think it's about nine miles. My footprints might still be on the trail; I know the trail well. I know the Foothill College track well, too. I ran there in the morning. Frost covered the pole-vault landing pit. My face was numb from the chilly air. People say running is healthy, but I nearly killed myself.

> *I don't know the title, call me greg*
> I don't know where I'm going,
> I don't know where I've been;
> I'm a wanderer
> Whose journey never ends.

I ate very little. A hard-boiled egg and two carrot sticks for dinner. No sugar at all. I weighed more in seventh grade than I did my freshman year. My birthday was not normal. My mom made a birthday cake for me. It was an oat-bran cake with honey. I told her to make me a healthy cake. There were a few weekends before the collapse that hinted at the future. I was so starved and exhausted that I ate lots of food and lay on the couch all day.

Monday morning, I ran for a couple of hours and forced myself to school. I refused to slow down even though my parents and friends told me to; I was a machine. I don't recall much of my life outside of wrestling and running and eating. Scales were a large part of my life. I remember watching the balance needle bounce up and down and hoping it would stop. I weighed ninety-nine pounds at one time. One time I ran up and down the bleachers at lunch time. Everyone stared at the crazy guy who ran at lunch time. I didn't realize what I was doing. I couldn't stop and take a deep breath and relax; everything was go, go, go.

For a long time, I never made contact with people other than my parents and counselors. I ate, and the more I ate, the more I gave up. There was a time when I was so far down that I enjoyed it. I looked at life from different angles. I went to summer school that summer. I said a lot of weird things. I thought about the universe a lot. "Who am I?" I wondered.

> *gertrude smith (gertrude is my grandma's name,*
> *grandpa calls her gerty)*
> Who am I?
> Am I
> Just a fly
> On a wall
> Hoping that I don't fall?

It was frustrating trying to rebuild my life. At times I was impatient. I took the all-or-nothing approach. No gradual climbing out of my hole; I was going to jump out all at once. I was going to change the world. There was a time when I thought everyone was stupid except me. I thought: "War is bad. People are hurt and some die. Am I the only one who realizes that war is not a good idea?!"

Self-Destruction
Lemmings march forward
Into the water.
Cows stand in line
For the slaughter.
Humans build the path
Into trouble,
And just laugh.

I hated going to psychiatrists. I didn't want any help because that would prove that I couldn't help myself. The mornings were the worst part of the day. I got up and pounded the walls and yelled. I kicked things and mumbled and stomped. My dad checked out the movie *The Great Race* from the library. Tony Curtis and Jack Lemmon watched me from the other side of the television screen.

For a while the TV was my only escape. It distracted me from reality and gave me simple, but temporary, pleasures. I went right from breakfast to the family-room couch. I became a regular watcher of the morning talk-shows. Sometimes I just ignored my parents when they talked to me. I covered my face with a pillow and pretended that they weren't there. I remember hating medication.

I wrote a note one day. My mom thought it was a suicide note. Actually, the note was a farewell note. I wrote that I was running away to Washington, D.C. to become President. I was going to end war and save the world. I said, "I'll be back in twenty years." I wanted to get away. I wanted to go away and live alone, survive a great struggle and come back refreshed. I wanted to go on a vision quest in the woods without food and find a purpose for life. I wanted to run away. But, also I wanted to stay home. I wasn't able to decide, so I did nothing.

During Winter Break, our family went to the Grand Canyon for a week. That was the first time I had left the house in a couple of weeks. It was hard.

I remember Phoenix and some cacti. One day, I refused to leave the hotel room when everyone went sightseeing.

I can't write. I feel strange and it is hard to remember. Exactly two years ago today, I had a seizure. The seizure was caused by my doctor's error. I was taking *Norpamine*, which wasn't the right drug for me to begin with. Then he added *Prozac*. The *Prozac* and *Norpamine* had a chemical reaction which gave me the seizure.

My dad bought me two computer games. My mind needed something to soothe it, like computer games or TV. I remember that I was playing *Joe Montana Football* on the computer. I walked into the kitchen to get something to eat. My dad told me later that I fell on the floor and started shaking and twitching. He said that it lasted for about thirty seconds.

When I got up I couldn't talk. I tried to talk, but no words came out. I had hallucinations of spiders dancing towards me. They were green and got bigger and bigger.

> *The BOMB*
> Everything was calm.
> Then came a bomb.
> And everything was gone.
> Good-bye and so long.

My dad had called an ambulance because he didn't have a car to drive me to the hospital. The ambulance came and the paramedics stuck oxygen tubes up my nose, and then I could talk. They also put an IV needle in the front of my forearm. The needle fed glucose into my veins. At the hospital my brain got scanned. I lay down on a board and they slid me into a huge tube. They couldn't find anything wrong with me, the medicines just had a chemical reaction and that caused the seizure.

I remember the mental hospital in San Jose. My parents literally dragged me there. I was clinging to doorways in my bathrobe screaming and crying. My parents had packed an overnight bag for me. My dad carried my shoes in his hand. They are abandoning me, I thought. The hospital checked me for razor blades and lice. The person who checked my hair suggested shampoos to get rid of my dandruff. The shower I took there was the first one I had taken in months. There was a net like the ones used for tightrope walkers below all the upstairs windows. The building was a square with a hole in the middle. The net was where the hole was. The windows facing the outside were barred.

I received a small tour when I arrived. The guide showed me a room with no windows. The room was solid steel. It was called the *Quiet Room*. The hospital put people in there who were angry and who wanted to yell. The room was soundproof, so a person could yell as loud as they wanted. The room scared me; the hospital scared me; it all felt so foreign. But life inside the hospital could not compare to what I was going through inside my head.

There were many times when I resolved to change, to get up and take a shower. Sometimes at night while lying in bed, I would say to myself, "Tomorrow, it's going to turn around. Tomorrow, I'll take life by storm." But, it didn't happen. I was impatient. It was hard to deal with a slow, gradual recovery.

Mornings were the worst. I'd wake up and see that my life was the same. I had the same feeling every morning. I hated the sunshine. There was light outside, but nothing inside. Mornings are supposed to be new beginnings, but mine were reminders of my pitiful existence.

When I returned home from the hospital, my dad and mom desperately wanted me to see a psychiatrist. "I don't need help! I'm better!" was my usual argument.

My dad countered, "Well, then I guess you're well enough to go to school tomorrow." For that I had no retort. That hurt me.

School was the kicker, the final step. The step before school was making contact with friends. I didn't have many close friends. I had acquaintances, but no one came to visit me. I was glad for that because I didn't want to be bothered. Part of me wanted to sulk around the house forever. At the same time I wanted to recover, but I didn't know how, and I was scared.

I knew basically what I needed to do. I needed to go outside. I needed to take a hike in the park, maybe shoot some baskets. And maybe, just maybe, if I had enough courage, I could call a friend. Or maybe answer the phone. I never answered the phone. I didn't want to talk to anybody I knew.

> I hear the sounds of a dismal drizzle,
> My plans for basketball just fizzle.
> I shouldn't pout,
> We need water to end the drought.
> Why can't it rain another day?
> A day when I'm too sick to play.

I went to a Spanish tutor for a while. I felt like an outcast. I quarantined myself. It was hard to get back in the swing of things after being out for so long. Getting back was like going on stage. I needed the mentality of a performer. "Go out there and do it," I thought.

I came back to school my sophomore year. I acted in *A Midsummer Night's Dream* and I also acted *life*. Sometimes I had stage fright and I stayed home and didn't want to be on stage. I wore sweat pants and a sweat shirt every day. I slept in my clothes and I never brushed my teeth. I remember eating raisin toast with peanut butter. I watched Regis and Kathy Lee and all the other morning talk shows. When I was really out of it, I watched soap operas.

> *Brainlessness is Bliss*
> I think I'll put my brain in a glass jar
> And throw it somewhere really really far.

Away from me
My brain would be.
Yeah, it would be cool
To be a complete fool,
Unaware
Without a care.
And I wouldn't have to worry
About wearing clean underwear.

My rear ached from sitting on the couch. My once strong legs had become jelly from being inactive. I had disintegrated not only mentally but physically as well.

I had no facial expressions. I looked at myself in the mirror. I smiled to see what it would look like. I grouped my experience in one glob that I called: *the depression*. Now I'm trying to break down the general term and understand myself more deeply.

One day my mom asked me to help her move plastic garbage bags full of leaves to the front of the house. "What if anyone sees me? I don't want to be seen!" I thought. I told my mom, "I can't. I just can't do it." I couldn't leave the safety of the couch, the TV, and the solitude.

Eventually, I dragged myself outside. I complained and worked slowly. It felt strange, real strange. It was the first time I had broken a sweat for a long time, aside from sweating out of anxiety or panic. I should have been proud of myself. I was proud to some extent, but I was also afraid.

I began doing things. I needed to move again. Everything took effort. Nothing came easy. My mom took my pulse once and it was pumping ninety beats a second. My dad tried to do some meditation with me, but I resisted. I tried to relax, but I was too tense.

I struggled to go to school. I was enrolled in regular classes and I was taking *Zoloft* a lot, so I was pretty high most of the time. Still I struggled. One day, a group of students came into my English class and made a presentation. They said I could learn more about myself and take charge of my own education. It was something different from the regular school. After sitting at home for so long doing nothing, I needed something that I could plunge into—The Learning Community sounded like a good way.

After coming out of my depression, I was feeling idealistic and wanted to change the world and grab something, do something. But I was still afraid because it was something new to me. It was hard for me to go to orientation meetings. My parents went before I did. When I finally attended a meeting, I was impressed by the closeness of the group, so I thought I might as well give it a shot. I enrolled for my junior year and stayed in the program for two years.

After school started, I was just there. I didn't go up to people and make friends. I was especially glad that no one tried to force me to do something or say something or be something. I was able to spend a lot of the time just watching and getting used to things.

> *My path*
> High on a plateau,
> I gaze down below
> On the path I have traveled.
> Oh, how my life has unraveled!
> Like a ball of string,
> Twisted,
> Turned,
> Around everything.

As I watched people the first few days, I got to know what they were like. They were all so different, yet the same. Andy loved to play basketball and he was really caring of others. Joe liked to ride his bike and hike in the mountains. Janna was really wise, really easy going, and I never felt out of place with her. Tamika brought laughs and light—light that I saw outside myself and wanted within.

I was happy just sharing the feelings of warmth and togetherness in the group. I liked our two-day retreat at Venture Lodge. I liked the simple things—like preparing meals and eating together, sitting out on the deck in the evening, standing outside in the morning in the fog. It might sound strange, but I liked going to sleep on the floor in a big room with a bunch of people at night and waking up together the next morning. It made me feel closer.

I remember Jenny's and Wendy's story of coming to the United States from El Salvador. I admired the struggle they had gone through and was interested in their history. I remember how good a listener Wendy was and how easy she was to talk to.

I liked Joe. I shared his interest in the outdoors; I went hiking with him a couple of times after school. One time we joined Kristie in the foothills near our school to help plant oak trees in a reforestation project. We were sent to look for acorns that could be planted. We didn't find any, but we had a good talk. I remember I talked to Joe about his summer trip to Idaho with the Student Conservation Group. He said he chopped a lot of wood; he also told me about a book he had read—*Dharma Bums* by Jack Keroac. I borrowed it and read it.

Paki and I just happened to connect at the EV's (Environmental Volunteers) meeting. I liked Paki; he was so mature and friendly and accepting. We teamed up to teach science lessons to little kids at Beechwood School, an all-black elementary school in East Menlo Park. Paki and I were two tall, skinny white guys; I guess we were quite a sight walking up to that school. When the kids saw us coming down the hall, they would all jump up and down and yell in excitement. They really liked us and it wasn't long before they gave us nicknames, ones that stuck with us for the next few months that we taught there—Beavis and Butthead. I liked the kids and I felt that we were doing something really useful there. Paki was the straight man and I taught using goofy characters that I made up. When we taught about birds, I painted my elbow like a big beak and pranced around like big crow.

> *Technology scares me. Well, what really scares me is that my brother has fused with the computer. I'm afraid that the whole human race will fuse with technology and existence will be incomplete without computers. I've always wanted to be a clown. I want to go to little kids' birthday parties and juggle and make a fool of myself.*

Sometimes, in our high school classroom, we would take time away from our usual discussions about the world to talk about ourselves. I liked the safety of our class; I could really be myself and no one judged me. Sometimes we would meet in small support groups outside the classroom after school. A support group is a group of four or five Learning Community students who help each other emotionally and academically and also have a good time. The small group makes our larger group more cohesive. We can take the time to get closer, to communicate, and to care about one another. Tamika was in my support group and I had special feelings for her—but she didn't know.

> *Now or never / gerG htimS*
> *Maybe it was the peculiar tasting Mountain Dew I guzzled at Taco Bell. Or maybe it was the phase of the moon or some wacky astrology thing. Whatever the reason, today was a strange day. A strange, but a good day. Today was a Saturday, and it began just like every Saturday of my young life. I stumbled out of bed and staggered into the kitchen. I then proceeded to inhale enough waffles to wallpaper Buckingham Palace. Still asleep I collapsed on the family room couch. I surfed through the channels in search of cartoons. "Hello today we are going to learn to cook a duck à l'or orange,"... flip! "Cobra Commander! The Joes are attacking headquarters in quadrant number seven!"... Uh, I don't think so ... flip!*

> *Today was a support group meeting. Tamika, Wendy, Andrea, and I decided to meet at Printer's Inc. It's a bookstore with a clever name that doubles as a*

coffee shop. I peddled my Peugeot to Tamika's house. I go everywhere on that bike. It gets about thirty miles per gallon—thirty miles-per-gallon of the soda that I drink. We cruised down El Camino in a car that looks like a large pregnant roller skate. In a unanimous decision, we agreed to stop at Taco Bell for some grub and beverages.

Wouldn't it be weird to be completely honest for a whole day. Like if your teacher asked you why you're late you would say, "I stopped to talk with a friend," instead of saying, "As we waited in the left turn, I watched an elderly man leaning on a walker, inching across the street. He moved like an inchworm, putting his walker six inches in front of him and then very slowly pulling himself to the walker. His process of motion was methodical and mechanical. He reminded me of an ancient machine, rusty and deteriorated, with the junk yard close in its future. Without warning, the man stopped. I could almost hear the wrenching and screeching of gears grinding to a halt."

"Give that man some oil!" I pleaded, for his gears could no longer mesh and turn without some lubrication. His stopping was contagious. Everyone ceased whatever they were doing and turned to stare at the frozen man in the crosswalk. He ignited a bolt of lightning, which flashed down my spine and into my soul. This bolt of lightning was the realization of my own mortality. Life is not something eternal. I could die at anytime. My adrenalin increased and I told myself to savor every moment."

Tamika was so *out there* all the time with her "Good morning, everybody!" I wanted to tell her what I thought of her, but I didn't know what to say to a girl. I had never had a crush on anyone before Tamika. One day, out of nowhere, I told her my feeling in front of the whole class. Tamika listened and said that she was touched by my words; no one made fun of me.

Untitled #7654: Call me Greg, my parents did.
I told her it was she
To whom I was attracted.
I had no expectations
On how she reacted.

The words
"I'm attracted to you,"
Came out of the blue and
I had no idea what to do.

Those words
Had been sitting on my shelf,
But when I said them
I surprised myself.

The Learning Community offered us a chance to build trust and overcome our fears. One of the ways that we did this was to take part in a ropes course. We took a bus several miles from school to the mountains. The place looked like a guerrilla encampment. Rope ladders hung from trees; logs and cables were suspended between trees fifty feet in the air; one tree was topped and had a small platform bolted to it. Rope belays hung everywhere. The people running the course wore hard-hats. They were inner city kids—boys and girls—enrolled in a continuation school near San Francisco. They were real supportive and friendly to us. We didn't know what to expect; our group was wide-eyed, intimidated by the height, but ready to climb! We spent several hours climbing trees and balancing on cables and logs suspended between trees. After a day of grueling, yet exciting activities, we approached our final group event.

I walked slowly along the trail; it was sprinkled with leaves, acorns, and snapping sticks. My left shoe was filled with dirt and I could feel it in between my toes. I took off my safety helmet and shivered as the wind chilled my sweaty scalp. I carried my helmet on my hip as an old lineman would after a grueling football game. We came upon a wall. Green wood, fifteen feet high, loomed over me. I joined the horseshoe of people forming at the base of the wall.

"Well here we are. The last event of the day, The Wall." For some reason the television show American Gladiators crossed my mind. Glenn, our instructor, sat on his haunches. He explained that, somehow, we had to get our whole

group over that wall. It was high. Our group came in all sizes; it didn't look as if we had a prayer to get our little band of players over that obstacle!

We had three minutes to plan. Then we were expected to do the entire event in silence. At first everyone tried to talk at once. Then Joe and Shawn concocted a plan. We would let them stand on our shoulders and form a human pyramid so that I could get to the top and then pull them up. From there Andy and Paki would direct the people on the ground, one-by-one, to be pushed and pulled to the top. Once we had our rhythm, people started up the wall—Alma, Paula, Mike, Jeremy, Andrea, and then Ali. Some of the bigger students were suspended in the air; we all stood below to spot our comrades—Janna, Angel, Joanna, Jenny, and Wendy all made it to the top. Soon it became clear that we were going to make it—Kristie, Adrienne, and Brenda were up and over. Oops, we almost forgot little Tamika—up and over she went!

We got so caught up in getting people up and over that we almost forgot how we were going to get Andy and Paki over. That was the hard part, Paki was last and had to back up, run toward the wall real fast, and leap with all his might. I barely caught his hand as I hung precariously from the top of the wall with my hands stretched out. "Caught him!" I said to myself, as the strain of his weight tested every muscle, tendon, and ligament in my right arm. Joe joined me in pulling Paki by the arm as he hung suspended over a sea of raised hands in case he fell. Then we felt Shawn's strength join ours and we knew we were going to succeed. Up came Paki and he scurried over the top of The Wall. I felt connected! I belonged! What joy! We had supported the entire group to a great moment of shared victory!

The kind of support and teamwork that our group created that day would be repeated over and over again throughout the entire year in our group's triumphs—in brainstorming, in our academic pursuits, in "interpersonals," in service.

Around Thanksgiving, I lapsed back into depression and stayed home for a few days. It was easier to come back to The Learning Community. I came on the day that we all went to Alma's to make tamales. Alma was from

Guatemala and her mother agreed to have the whole class come to their apartment so she could teach us how to make tamales. People were glad that I was back, but no one freaked out about my absences. I just fit back in. I felt comforted getting back with the group.

I learned a lot about a lot of things. Hard to say what or how, but looking back at myself before and after, Learning Community made a big impact on me. It was one of the first times I had had real heart-to-heart communication. I learned a lot about myself, given the opportunity. When we started the book-writing project, I got to write about myself. *I got to observe myself as well as be myself.* And when we read and discussed Rene Dumal's *Mt. Analogue*, I got into the symbolism so much that Gary had me lead the class discussions.

Support was the glue that held our group together. In one of our weekly "interpersonals," one of the students was sharing some painful experiences that she was having in her life. She got so emotional that she started to sob and to shake. Gary went over to her and stood behind her chair; he simply put his hands on her shoulders while he spoke to her; he seemed to calm her with supporting hands. I was surprised that he knew exactly what to do in the situation. After she had a chance to experience her emotions and the flood of feelings, we began to talk. Things became clear and, after a while, I could feel her healing in the circle. We were all a part of it. We were all there for her. As she healed, something healed in me—in each of us. I felt the process draw us closer as a group.

It was at that point that I realized just how caring humans could be. Also, I learned that when someone is down, he or she may simply need someone to be there for him or her. I realized that I could give another person this kind of support when he or she was having a tough time. This was an important lesson for me; this was something that I could do, just offer my hand or show someone love. It seemed so much more effective than giving psychological advice.

While my true face came out more and more in The Learning Community, I continued acting on stage. I got the part of David in *David and Lisa*. The story is about a young boy whose parents put him in a mental institution where he attends a school with other kids who are also having emotional problems. I felt close to the character and wanted to portray him as a *real* person. It was an easy role for me to play, although it was a little painful. David wasn't close to people; he was very isolated. He kept telling his parents and psychiatrist to get off his back. Playing the role of David was therapeutic for me. The experience was profound because I could share the character *and* myself with the audience. In many ways my actor's mask wasn't so foreign; maybe it was less of a mask than the audience knew.

David finds his recovery by working with others. He begins to relate to his psychiatrist as a friend. Then he falls in love with a girl, Lisa, who has a split personality. Through her, he gets over his fear of physically and mentally touching people. Eventually Lisa runs away from the institution; David goes out and finds her being harassed by some boys. The play ends with David and Lisa returning to the mental institution hand-in-hand. Playing David was the exploration of another mask for me: a vulnerable teenager, acting in a role, and pretending to be a vulnerable teenager. My parents came to the play and supported me. So did my friends in the Learning Community.

The ending of the play reminded me of our Learning Community "interpersonals." I always felt good whenever we had interpersonals and could support each other. I felt connected with everyone when things got resolved. It was satisfying for me to witness other people as they grew to understand and accept themselves. It was healing for me to feel the support of the group. Before Learning Community, I was just a lonely robot that no one could understand. It was impossible for me to know who I was. I couldn't express myself. I couldn't be myself.

Through my experiences in The Learning Community, I was able to express myself and show compassion for others. People listened. They accepted me. I learned that I am not completely alone in the world; other people out there understand me. *I am not alone*. When I could reach out and feel a connection with others, I gained the confidence to look inside. I recognized that *knowledge is inside me*—the sense of my inner knowledge feels like a wise old man. Even when I am unable to express it in the moment, I know it is there. Now I know that I have a greater wisdom inside me. In it lies my true face.

Passage Four:
Empowering Ourselves

Fighting for a Place to Stand

Shawn

It started out as a fairly normal day for me. The usual stuff—almost sleeping through my alarm, mom nagging me about picking up the dirty clothes that I wore at Andrea's garden yesterday and dumped by the doorway, and having to pump my bicycle tires so I could make it to school on time. Oh yeah, and dreading having to show up at class once again without my homework.

I got to class just before the tardy bell rang and sat down in one of the chairs in the circle of our classroom. I looked up at our three-week calendar to see what we were going to do today and discovered that we were going to be discussing the election initiatives.

We started our day with students making announcements and organizing details for coming events—fund raising activities, transportation for field trips, and information on speakers in the community. Andy, in charge of the Mexicali service project fundraiser, announced that we had to raise $200 more before we reached our goal of $2000. Kristie said it would cost $450 to use a school bus for the San Francisco modern-art field trip; she wondered whether we might be able to invite some parents to drive. Adrienne announced a one-man show at Fort Mason performed by Ron Jones; she wondered if we wanted to go as a group Friday night. Paki announced a book-reading by Liz Dana, the daughter of Elizabeth Duvenek, a local activist and founder of Peninsula School (which he and Kristie had attended) and Hidden Villa (where Joe volunteered in the garden). It was organizational stuff that usually punctuates the beginning of our day. But, as it turned out, today wasn't going to be a typical day.

Wendy interrupted the announcements by blurting out, "I'm really upset about something that happened yesterday." She started to cry, but she pushed on, "Some people in the group have been out of commitment and I think that they should speak for themselves about it."

I could tell by the look on her face and the trembling in her voice that something was really bothering her. I wasn't really in the mood for emotional discussions today, so I got a bit annoyed and wondered, "Now what the hell is eating her today!"

Things got silent in the room; I looked around. Evan and Andrea were looking down at the floor. Some of the students were looking at me. A cold feeling came over me as I thought, "Oh, oh! Now I know what's up." I folded my arms as if to protect myself and settled back into the chair."No one is gonna get me," I decided, as I glanced over my shoulders as if to protect my flanks. Then I pretended to stare off into a poster at the far end of the room.

My mind flashed back to the group's garden project. Over the past few Saturdays, some of our group members—Greg, Janna, Joanna, and Andrea—had taken organic gardening classes at a local ecology center. The group taught the rest of us some of the techniques during class. Our group's goal was to learn how to grow vegetables in a way that had the least impact on the Earth. After we understood what we needed to do, we assigned the group to five garden sites at students' houses so we could experiment with the farming methods.

Yesterday, my group was to prepare the soil at Andrea's house. That was the plan anyway; but we happened to pick a miserably hot day. To make matters worse, the soil was really packed at Andrea's and it hadn't been worked for years.

I didn't feel like working too hard in the heat, but I dug in and worked up a pretty good sweat. Evan and Andrea were part of my garden group. They felt pretty much the same way I did, and it wasn't too long before we were standing around sharing our misery. Evan suggested that it might be easier to work if we took a break and smoked some weed to ease the pain. Andrea agreed and went inside the house in search of her private stash. When she returned, we sat down in the shade and smoked a joint.

I hadn't given our actions a second thought yesterday. Now, I was sitting in class and Wendy is pissed!

I maintained my silent, defensive posture—arms folded, eyes straight ahead. As other students began to speak up, I realized that the word was out, but it seemed that no one was going to point the finger at me. "They better not." I thought, "Nobody better mess with me!"

I quickly checked my options. My natural instinct was to put up my guard, quietly at first, then if someone accused me, to deny any involvement loudly and indignantly. If they pressed me, I would say, "It's none of your goddamn business what I do off campus." Then if people persisted, I'd just walk out. "Nobody's going to mess with me," I thought as I renewed my vow of silent defiance.

Finally, Andrea spoke up, "Well, I smoked a little marijuana at my house while we were working on the garden yesterday. It was my fault, you guys."

"DAMN!" I thought, "She didn't have to say anything. Wendy wasn't going to rat on us and now Andrea is admitting it."

About that time, Evan said, "Well, I did it, too."

"Now, we are really in trouble," I thought, " The class knows, Gary knows, and we are really going to get it."

So I tried to discount it, "OK. So I did it too; but we weren't in school and it wasn't even enough to get high on." That created quite a stir.

Janna reminded me, "You gave your word to be drug-free before and during all class activities, just like the rest of us did. You know you were involved in an LC project."

Wendy got really choked up again and said, "Shawn, when I gave my word to the group at he beginning of the year, I meant it, and I trusted everyone to keep their word, too. Now, I can't trust the group anymore."

Greg jumped in and pointed out, "We need to address specific people. The *group* is made up of twenty-five different people." He made it clear what his intentions were, "I'm still going to keep my commitments. Could we please talk directly to each other, instead of talking *at* the group?"

Kristie looked right at me, so directly that I couldn't look away and stated, "Do you realize what you have done? You've broken your word to us."

I wanted to blow her off. Actually, I wanted to fight someone (not her) or run (I wasn't sure where). But the way she talked to me was so direct that I couldn't blow her off, I wanted to, I just couldn't. Here she was asking me why I hadn't kept my word to myself—and to the group. I needed to think about this one. I finally blurted out "I just wasn't thinking." It was the truth, I hadn't thought about it. I just acted in the moment, did what I felt like at the time, and now the whole dammed group was on my case. "Besides," I added, "a little pot was no big deal." I was still fighting for my position in the group.

Andrea looked over at me as if she had realized something really important. This was her second year in the program. The first year she had had a lot of problems with drugs. She said that the group had really helped her a lot. When she came into the group she had been doing drugs every day and had claimed that it didn't affect her mental state, so she didn't think it mattered if she did them. Somehow in that first year she had turned around. "No Shawn," she said, "there is more to it than that. I wasn't thinking either, but I know it was wrong. We gave our word in the beginning of the year, and we broke it. That *does* mean a lot to me!" Then she started crying—something that I had never seen her do before.

Evan, the newest member of our group, looked up and shared his thoughts, "All right, we broke a commitment. I'm sorry. But, what do you want us to do? It already happened." His sarcastic tone gave away his impatience. I thought he might get up and leave. I just might have joined him, too.

"What do *you* want to do about it?" Adrienne countered. Then the group got silent again.

The discussion lasted for over an hour. I was challenged when I got reactive, or defensive, or started to sound like a victim. I was supported when I was vulnerable, painfully honest, or took responsibility for myself. I looked around at the class; many of the students had confronted difficult issues in their lives during the school year. The group members asked them to be responsible for themselves; they became stronger and our group became stronger. I began to realize that my smoking dope at the garden somehow had affected the whole group. I realized that my everyday behavior didn't necessarily lead me to things that were best for me, either, because I liked these people and I wanted to be part of this group. Somehow, my standing up and being responsible for my actions and living up to my word helped make the group to be what it was.

"Wow, this is new stuff for me," I thought to myself. It wasn't easy to be fully honest—especially with myself. It was weird to have my classmates call me on my actions and it was weird not to react, not to get defensive, not to want to fight, or not to want to bail.

Somewhere in the discussion Jenny said, "I care about you and I want you to care about yourself." She must have gotten to me. I really wanted to be here. I didn't want to withdraw, fight, or run.

And then when Kristie repeated Adrienne's question, "What do *you* want to do about it?" I was really taken off guard. I was both surprised and lost. Throughout my life, whenever things had gotten heated, I had always tried to get out of the trouble that I was in. I never took responsibility for what I did, never set up consequences for my actions, and never learned from the situations.

The group's persistence, and now its silence, caused me to reflect. Then Evan, Andrea, and I joined in a three-way conversation in the group. I was confused, so I asked them what we could do. Andrea looked for some kind of authority, "There must be some school rule that applies," she said. She turned to Gary and asked, "What are you required to do as the teacher?"

He seemed fairly neutral. It was obvious, earlier in the group confrontation, that he wasn't happy about what we had done, but he hadn't pressed anything and he seemed content to let us figure it out. He replied, "Well, if I had caught you with drugs or caught you smoking pot, I would have been bound by my responsibility as a teacher to turn you over to the administration, immediately. I might have been moved to take further action that would have jeopardized your position in the group, since you broke your commitment to the group. But, since members of the group brought this issue out in the open, I think that you need to resolve it as a group."

I looked back at Evan and Andrea and said, "So, I guess the three of us are going to have to work this one out ourselves." A sense of sadness came over me. I said, "I really feel shitty! God, I'm really sorry that I let you guys down."

Gary replied, "I, for one, don't want you to *feel guilty*. I want you to *be responsible*." He added, "Guilt can becomes its own reward, if you feel badly without changing anything."

Evan, Andrea, and I talked to each other while the group listened. We talked about consequences. Maybe we should have to put in more time working in the garden, maybe we could dig other groups' plots for them this weekend. We explored other ideas, but found it hard to shake the feeling of having done something to the group.

Finally, Evan said he had been thinking of leaving the group. Andrea picked up on this idea immediately, "Maybe we don't deserve to be in the group anymore. Maybe we should all leave the group."

Wendy, who had been silent since her emotional plea earlier, came alive. She leaned forward on the edge of her chair and pointed at each of us. "If you guys leave, I'd really be pissed! I want you in our group, not out. Think about what we've been through, what we've created together, and what we've planned to do this year." Others quickly added their agreement to Wendy's statement. The will of our group was certainly against our leaving.

"God, it's so hard," I thought, "A few months ago, it would have been so much easier. I would have just gotten up, told everyone to 'go to hell' and walked out. I think that Evan and Andrea would have walked out too. And now, that doesn't even feel like an option."

Finally, after a lot of soul searching and much discussion, we came up with a solution that seemed right for us, and one that the group supported as well. We decided to do three things. First, we would re-commit to our group's agreements. Second, we would do our part to make the group work for the remainder of the year. The final step in our solution seemed real different: the three of us would get up, walk to the vice principal's office, explain what we had done, and willingly accept the school's consequences. The entire solution was our idea and we chose to do it of our own free will.

Various members of the group counseled us on which vice principal we should go to—we chose Mrs. Hammel. Then we walked to her office and sat down. One by one, each of us told her what we had done. She was astonished. As we completed our explanation by saying that we were ready to accept the consequences, she was even more surprised. She said that she had never had a student come to her asking to be punished before. She told us that she admired us for what we had done and would like to send us back to class without further consequence, confident that we had learned a valuable lesson without any coercion from the institution. "But," she said, "the school board policy requires that students who use drugs during school activities must be suspended for three days. It is my commitment to the school to follow its rules."

She did soften our punishment by saying, "Today will count as one day, tomorrow as the second day and, if you will report to my office at 7 a.m. on the morning of the third day, you will not have to miss class that morning."

As I walked off campus to begin my suspension, I thought about the person that I had been—the guy looking for a place in which to belong, the hold-back kid, the playing-it-safe guy, the prize fighter who always kept an eye on the exits, the guy that never quite fit in. This really wasn't the person that I wanted to be. I had felt more strength, personal power, and sense of belonging today than I had ever felt in my life. I could be open and honest, I could listen to others in the group, and I could feel that I was part of the moment that we all built together. As for exits, the only door that I was interested in was the one the whole group would pass through, and that was the one that led us all into the future together.

It wasn't easy though. Even though our group had shared special moments and pulled together to work our way through obstacles, for me—and for some of the others—the experience still felt incomplete. We knew that we couldn't feel fully in charge until we got our personal studies under control. But control was something that I had fought so hard against most of my life—especially in school.

I didn't want to be somewhere if I thought I was being controlled. My style was to play a game of Cat-and-Mouse with the teacher and the class. The challenge for me was to find the easiest way out, to discover how to get around the teacher's rules, or to join the class rebels and find ways to sabotage the teacher's lessons or teacher's authority. It wasn't so much that I wanted to be destructive; it was just that I didn't like to be controlled. When I don't have control over my circumstance, the game is to find ways not to be compliant, not to cooperate.

When I first came into LC, I didn't really believe that Gary meant it when he said we were going to *co-create* the course; actually I didn't really understand it because I had never done it before. But when I began to understand what we were up to, I honestly saw an opportunity to do nothing. When Gary suggested that we had an opportunity to create anything we wanted, my inner conversation was, "Good, I don't like school, so I won't do anything."

As I heard other students coming up with ideas of what we cold do, I found some of their ideas intriguing and took part in some of their discussions, but I still held back, didn't initiate, and didn't do any research outside of school.

I tested Gary's philosophy. "If we are in charge and we can do whatever we want, then why can't I do nothing or just hang out with my friends and listen to music and stuff," I thought. Well, that's what I did for quite a while. Gary didn't get mad at me; I wasn't punished or belittled in class. The only problem was that, the way the class was structured, I wasn't getting the courses and credits that I needed to graduate. I wrote a contract, but I hadn't turned in any course work, and when Gary and I met every other week for our thirty-minute evaluation conference, I didn't have any work to show him. We would just talk about me or my interests outside of school. Sometimes we talked about my plans for the future. But, as glorious as my dreams were, they weren't working. I couldn't lie. I couldn't fabricate things or fill in worksheets the last minute—I just hadn't done the work. Gary didn't push me to do it; I know that he wanted me to work, but he said that it wouldn't help if he wanted it more than I did. Still, he saw my lack of progress and somehow I wanted him to see something different from me.

It was hard to rebel against myself. The message I was getting from Gary was: "This is your life. What do you want to do with it?" It took quite a while for this message to sink in. Yes, it was my life, but I had been running away for so long that I didn't know what I wanted to run toward. I could set up personal goals for myself, but I had to think this one through. What did I really want? If it was high school graduation that I wanted, the school had external standards for me. If it was college that I wanted, colleges had entrance requirements. But I needed something much more relevant to my life to build my goals around. The best I could do for now was to focus on who I was and what the world was all about.

In the end, it was up to me. I had the choice to determine what I would do and how I would do it. The group had the same opportunity. It took a long time to realize that that seemed to be the purpose of our program: to discover our own way, then do it. But it was hard to shed old ways. After all, I had had ten years to develop my current attitude about school and old habits fall hard. I noticed some change as I went through the school year, and I knew that I wanted to have a good life. So I began to seek my way, and not just hang out.

My stubbornness and laziness slowly gave way to just going along with the program and listening to others. As the year progressed, I found that I started to make suggestions during our planning sessions and people listened to my ideas. I even started getting interested in what was going on in the world and discussing it. It was cool to find out about things and to see what principles my opinions were based on. I began to understand how other people made choices and why they did the things they did; I began to see my own actions as products of my own choices. I started to feel like this world was my world, that I had some stake in the it, and that I could, in some small way, change it. These were startling discoveries for the class "prize fighter with his eyes on the exits."

Our four-hour-per-day class gave us enough time to know each other personally and to care about each other. It also gave us the time to have in-depth discussions and really find out what people believed and cared about. We respected each other so we spent the time to understand each other. Discussions ended when we had shared all the points of view of a topic, not when somebody won and somebody else lost. The emphasis was on understanding the issue, understanding our values, challenging our assumptions, and seeking the truth. I liked that; it gave me a different view of school, not because those same classroom goals didn't exist elsewhere, but because we discovered and created them for ourselves.

We did get some help. Gary conducted a four hour Psychological Systems seminar each week. In the beginning of the year he helped us to get to know and trust each other. After we began to work together more effectively, he had us look deeper into who we were. We learned how to take greater interpersonal risks and challenge each other to keep our word. We looked at our values and how we made choices in life. One of the systems that he presented, Kohlberg's System of Moral Reasoning, became a model for us during the year in evaluating and making our choices. We learned that people make decisions based on how they see the world. We explored the kind of decision-making that results from self-indulgence, rewards and punishment, back-scratching, approval, duty, contract, and principle. Since we had started our year by agreeing to a set of commitments, our challenge was to base our decisions on our group contract. Then, as we investigated our personal values, we began to apply our principles to our decision-making. We applied these lessons as we worked out our issues as Andrea, Evan, and I did with the garden issue or as we discussed global issues.

Circumstances in the group helped me see that I could make more out of my life. I realized that the game of Cat-and-Mouse that I had played could be replaced by real learning with real people who cared about each other. Working together to make a difference in the world was far more entertaining and meaningful than just hanging out and doing nothing. With each new experience, our class became more like real life, rather that school. I had learned a new way to gain acceptance. Now I really felt like I belonged in a way that I had never felt before. Defiance and rebellion had been replaced by a stronger bond. I had found a place where I could stand: *I had chosen to stand on principle*. As I took my stand, I found that I was not alone. Our group had found a common strength, one that was based on principle and one that we could develop together.

On the Road to Citizenship

Jenny

I have early childhood memories of streets, roads, and seemingly endless highways. My family was always going somewhere, somewhere that offered a better way or a better life, a place that offered peace and understanding.

I was born in El Salvador, a country torn apart by a bloody civil war. I suffered the chaos of my country as a small child. The suffering was so deep that the images of the war were pushed from my conscious mind. The pain prevented me from remembering my childhood. My parents' strength during those traumatic times helped my brother, my sisters, and me survive. They have helped me retrieve some of those memories. Now I need to relive those events so that I can free myself and move on. I am the person that I am today because of the experiences that I have endured. As my parents have helped me recall the events of the past, I have been able to gain a greater appreciation for the value of my culture and for the value of my life.

In the mid 1970s, people were still prosperous in El Salvador. My grand-parents owned a small restaurant; my dad worked in a big fancy hotel in San Salvador and attended the university; my mom sold cut flowers in her small shop. My brother played ball with kids in the neighborhood and my sister was just learning to talk. Our family had a new baby in the house—they named me Jenny. The *gringos* from the north brought big tourist dollars into our country. People spoke proudly of the crowning of El Salvador's own as Miss Universe in 1976. We were a small country that depended on other countries for many of our needs, but we were a hard-working people. Life was simple. Then things began to change.

In the seventies, as now, fourteen families owned ninety-eight percent of the land and controlled the economy. They, especially, enjoyed the fruits of the prosperous seventies. While the masses wanted land reform, those in power wished to hold onto the status quo.

My family was poor. We were descendants of the great Maya civilization that built great pyramids, developed a calendar, and created an advanced systems of mathematics. When the Europeans came five hundred years ago, the Maya civilizations had crumbled and my people were left to toil in the fields for their colonial masters. In recent times, the ruling class has been wealthy upper-class *Mestizos* (mixed ancestry) and people of European descent. Indigenous people, like my family, had to struggle.

In the late '70s, a guerrilla war broke out. At first bankers and businessmen were kidnapped and held for ransom to fund the peasants' revolt. Fearing for their safety, big cruise ships carrying wealthy tourists quit coming to El Salvador. The economy suffered. Dad lost his job—no *gringos*, no jobs. Businesses closed; wealthy Salvadoreans began depositing large sums of money in Swiss bank accounts. Escalation of guerrilla activity in the countryside prompted a heavy response from the government. Army troops conducted a country-wide crackdown on anything that looked like a rebellion by the peasant population. By 1980, a full-scale civil war had begun.

Before the war, we lived in a modest home, but when my dad lost his job, we had to live in a small room that was sub-divided so that other families could share the house. Everyone used the same bathroom, kitchen, and yard. Soldiers with guns used to come to our house looking for young men to conscript. My sister, Wendy, was only four but she remembers that, as they passed through our yard, we asked, "Are you here to knock on our door or are you going to kill us?"

These questions were not the product of children's fantasies. My mother recalls many times that we were in the wrong place at the wrong time. Sometimes we were walking to the market when suddenly gun shots rang out on both sides of us. She had nowhere to run, so she huddled in a corner of a building to protect my brother and sisters. She drew us together, hugged us tightly, and used her body to cover us like a shield. We waited until the gunshots died down and the skirmish was over; then, as we were leaving, we saw signs of the madness that had taken place. The streets were littered with dead bodies; the day was as silent as the night. My mother tells me that I used to point out where the lifeless bodies were lying and count them as we walked back home. I was a typically curious child, taking in the world around me like a giant unfolding movie. But my natural curiosity didn't protect me from the harshness of my surroundings. I was not equipped to understand what my small-child eyes took in; nor did I know enough to look away from a sight that a small child should not see.

My father had been unemployed for one year. He took care of us kids when my mother was at work at the floral shop. Sometimes he went to the university; that was where everyone shared the news about what was happening in the country. Sometimes teachers and students didn't come to school because they feared they would be killed. One time in San Marcos, we were on a bus and some soldiers made us stop and get out. They made us file past a pointed stick that had a school teacher's head impaled on it. Sometimes, soldiers even killed teachers in front of their students.

My mother was a devout Catholic. She attended Bishop Romero's church in San Salvador. Romero openly supported the plight of the poor people. When my mother couldn't attend the masses, she listened to his daily broadcast of the religious services. The day Romero was assassinated my mother was home. She went to San Salvador to attend his funeral services. During the services the army opened fire on mourners in the town square who hadn't been able to get into the already packed church. She was among the anguished people running everywhere looking for cover. The next day my dad found piles of shoes in the town square, left to represent the innocent victims of a cruel war. My father and mother desperately wanted to get us out of the country.

Mother's Day was a good time for my mother's flower business; also, it was a good time to make money for the trip north. Our family had worked hard and had saved two hundred dollars. This was enough to get my dad a passport, a bus ticket, and a visa to Mexico. His visa was difficult to get because government workers siphoned off most of the legal visas and sold them on the black market. Dad shared many tearful "good-byes" and left our village the day after Mother's Day.

Everything on his trip cost money. He even had to pay to cross the Guatemalan border. The soldiers wanted fifty dollars and threatened to send him back, so he waited for the night guard who insisted on only twenty dollars. From there he took several weeks to get through Mexico. He spent several days on busses and even longer periods waiting in small towns until the time was right. It was a long passage, and he took careful notes so that we could eventually follow the same path. After a long, hard journey, he reached the U.S. He lived with his sister in California and found a job. He sent money to us as often as he could. Our own journey had to wait; we would not follow for another year and a half. To complicate matters, mom had gotten pregnant just before my dad left.

During the long year-and-a-half, events didn't get any better in El Salvador. One day my mother was in a bus with my brother; someone threw a Molotov Cocktail at the bus and it became engulfed in flames. In the fury as everyone tried to escape, my mom became separated from my brother and he had to break a window to get out. Often when we accompanied my mom on the twenty-minute ride to her workplace, we saw soldiers in helicopters swoop down and shoot at people. Sometimes, in the big city of San Salvador there were plastic bags with body parts lying on the streets with blood oozing out of them.

Some memories weren't so gruesome, those I seem to remember without my mother's prompting. I remember when my brother's pet chicken died; we sang the guerrilla anthem over its grave. And then there was the night that my mom started to have labor pains. Martial law had been declared and the soldiers wouldn't let her go to the city. She insisted, so they drove her to the hospital in a big army tank.

Other images are harder to remember without my mother's prompting. She recalls grimly the time that she was walking through the market place with us kids. She had to grasp my hand real tight and tug on it to get me past the ugly and brutal sights left by the government's death squads the night before. My natural curiosity, once again, tugged back as we passed a dead body left in the street of our village, a symbol left there by sick-minded soldiers to warn our people against getting involved in the war. I wanted to stop and stare at the lifeless form lying limp on the street just a few feet away from where I stood. The blood from this young peasant oozed from a ragged hole in his chest and thickened as it formed little rivers of red in between the cobblestones at my feet. At the time, I was more curious than shocked; now, I shudder and cringe.

The dead boy was like so many others in our village and from villages like ours throughout El Salvador. Yet, he seemed so still, and the vacant expression on his face seemed to cry for comfort. The flies that crawled across his open eyes and into his nostrils and open mouth had no under-standing or compassion for this young man—his passion for life, the family he left behind, the land or freedom that he fought for, the desire to escape from poverty and oppression and brutality and death.

For years I effectively repressed the ugly memories of death as well as the sad "good-byes" that my mom, my brother, my sisters, and I made to our dad as he left us to flee to the north in search of a better life for our family. We repeated these difficult "good-byes" to our grandparents, aunts, and uncles, cousins, and friends months later when we had accumulated enough money to join my father in the United States. With his directions, we were able to follow the same long route to freedom that he had taken.

We boarded a bus for Guatemala, our first link to the long road to *el norte*. We were headed away from political repression, poverty, and war in El Salvador and toward freedom, abundance, and peace in the U.S. I remember the bus ride; mostly I remember snuggling around my mom and holding her tightly as if she were a rock in the middle of some kind of raging river. We boarded and unboarded many buses. My mother carried most of our possessions on her back. When Wendy got sick, she had to carry her, too. My brother and I had to take care of our little sister and carry the rest of the family possessions. We carried everything that we owned—things to sustain us along the way and things to give us a new start in our new home. All our other possessions had been given away to family and friends back home.

I remember the hum of the tires and the drone of the engine as the bus spewed diesel fuel behind us. Out of the window I saw green mountains—

the dense tropical rain forest of Guatemala. Thick mist clung to the tree tops around us. I remember the bus slowing down on mountain roads waiting for slow traffic or burros to get out of the way. We slept and ate on the bus, getting out only to change busses, go to the bathroom, or wait in a crowded station for a transfer.

At each stop, people crowded in to fill the bus and food vendors passed through the aisles to sell their wares. I remember the mangoes that we bought for pennies; they left my little sister's mouth and shirt covered with yellow juice and pulp. I remember seeing mountains and valleys changing shape as we wound our way northward. Even the colors and styles of clothing changed after we made our way through Guatemala, Chiapas, and Oaxaca to the central states of Mexico.

We pushed on up the road toward Mexico City. It seemed like an eternity, but the road became my teacher and I knew that every mile took me closer to my father and to my new home. Travel and being uprooted were new to me and I didn't know what to expect. I knew nothing of the difficulties that lay ahead—traveling hundreds of miles through Mexico, running out of money, waiting for more money to arrive, and finding a way to cross the Mexico-U.S. border.

"Where are we going?" we asked my mom whenever we got restless and impatient.

"To see your dad," she replied.

"When will we get there?" was our comeback.

"The one who will see your father is the one who will sleep," was always be her final refrain. And sleep we did.

After four days of non-stop travel, we arrived in Durango, Mexico. In order to cross the Mexican-U.S. border, it was important that we be seen as Mexican citizens. Central Americans would be suspected of emigrating and stopped. We stayed in Durango with some friends for a month while we acclimated to the mannerisms and language of Mexico. After traveling this far, we didn't want to get caught crossing at some border town and get sent all the way back to El Salvador. We borrowed our friends' Mexican birth certificates—these would be returned by mail after we were safely in the U.S. While staying in Durango, we had to sleep outside in a three-walled building; my face got discolored from the extreme cold temperatures at night, a dead give away that I was not from that region. My mother kept me out of sight.

In the Durango bus station, my mother got off the bus to buy us some food. While she was gone, the bus started up and left the station. In panic, my mother ran to catch the bus, but it left the station before she could catch up. Here we sat, my brother, sisters, and me, struck speechless as our mother ran behind the bus in city traffic. She cast aside her prized possessions that hung around her neck to increase her pace, almost catching up when the bus was delayed, then losing ground as the bus surged ahead as the pace quickened.

Finally, after about twenty minutes, she caught up with the bus and pounded on the door to get in. She had lost some of her possessions: our family pictures, milk bottles for my baby sister, extra clothes, shoes, our toys, identification papers, and money. When she got back on the bus, we didn't worry about what was lost. We were relieved and happy to be back together again. We all huddled together tightly, wondering if we would ever get to our new home.

After the bus incident, we could afford only three seats on the bus for the five of us. My mom even had to give up some of her meals for us. She got pretty thin during the rest of the trip from eating so little.

After we left Durango for Mazatlan we had a long, scary drive over mountains to the coast. Our bus driver told us that the route was called *El Paso de la Muerte* (The Path of Death). He explained that, if a bus went over the edge, the authorities would leave it where it fell, because the terrain was too steep and rugged to pull it out. Our family squeezed closer together at that thought. We passed through some of the mountain region at night. I remember that the full moon was so bright that we could look over the edge of the highway, way down into the canyon below. I remember saying, "*Es hondo, hondo, hondo, hondo,* ... (It's deep, deep, deep, deep, ...)" over and over to myself because, in spite of the intensity of the moonlight, I still couldn't see the bottom of the canyon.

From Mazatlan, the drive to Tijuanna took another three days. We had to wait there two weeks before we could arrange for a *coyote*—a person who helps smuggle non-citizens across the border—to take us into the U.S. We lived in a shack and had very little food or water. I remember that my mother crossed the border one day to make arrangements for us. I had to stay back with the woman who served as our *coyote* because my skin was so dark that I might be seen as a Central American and attract too much attention at the border. Many refugees were fleeing the war in El Salvador and the Border Patrol readily stopped people who looked like me.

Everyone I had ever known spoke of the goal of getting into the U.S. We would be safe there, and that thought comforted me. Finally the day came. I remember the exact moment that we crossed the border.

We traveled on to Los Angeles, we had to wait for two weeks for my dad to drive down from Sunnyvale in northern California to pick us up. My dad said that I didn't recognize him. It had been a year and a half since I had seen him. For a long time I just called him *tio* (uncle). The older men living in our house in El Salvador were my father's and mother's brothers, so I was used to calling men "uncle." I was not living with my uncles any more; this was my dad!

My mother and father wanted us to come to the United States so that we could be together in peace and could live better than we had among the horrors committed in El Salvador. To accomplish that dream, we had to live without my father for a year-and-a-half. My mother had to take her four children on a journey that lasted thirty-one days. Now we had arrived in the land of the rich, the land of opportunity, paradise. But the reality we encountered was different from the glorious stories we had heard.

When we arrived in Sunnyvale, we stayed in a house where ten other people lived. We were a family of six, so all together we filled the tiny two-bedroom house with sixteen people, half of them children. My mom recalls those days vividly. She told me that she hated living in such crowded quarters and often longed to return to her native country. We were very poor, but we still strived to make the best of it. As a family, we never asked for much, and what we had was enough. Our parents worked hard and saved their money, until we finally could afford a place of our own.

We left the Sunnyvale house behind, but the experience is still with me. Those sixteen people were my family, and every day their love nourished my growth. I've always felt very close to my family and my love for them is very special. My home has always been so full of love that I grew up never believing that we were poor. My parents made little things seem like the world to us; I thank them for that. They taught me to be grateful for everything I have. Material things are not what is important in the world.

We settled in Mountain View, California, and eventually we applied for and received legal status as permanent residents through the Amnesty Act. My brother, my two sisters, and I enrolled in school and we learned English quickly. Soon we were making a new home for ourselves in the U.S.

Much later, when I made a brief visit back to El Salvador, I found that the situation had not improved. In the night I could hear bombs and see sparks of light fly. The concussions kept me awake until dawn. My trip reminded me that I am very lucky to have gotten out.

School was another road for me. It was a road to success, to share in the abundance of the American culture. I studied hard and learned the language, got good grades, and entered high school. In some ways, I guess, traveling this road was easier for me than for my classmates. They already had the security of citizenship, I didn't. I saw what hard work and study might give me someday; they just took what they had for granted. I looked for special challenges along the way—I did extra work in school, volunteered to help the teacher, and looked for opportunities to advance myself.

When I got to high school my world grew even more as I realized how much there was to learn that didn't fit in the textbook. I was a skinny freshman lost in the halls of high school. I couldn't even remember where my classes were or where the bathroom was. I was forced into a world of independence because I had to work. Yet I felt lost between school and my job. I didn't feel that I belonged anywhere.

Then something special happened. I was invited to participate in a pilot program to help an existing program called The Learning Community expand. A lunch meeting was scheduled to discuss the "School of the Future." At that time, the subject didn't interest me, but the free lunch did. I went to that first meeting just to satisfy my hunger. To my surprise the meeting was not what I expected; by the time it was over, I felt excited by the concept of students being responsible for their own education. I decided to help work for the expansion of the program.

As we continued to meet during my freshman year, I grew to like the meetings and the people. In the end, the expansion did not go through and our pilot program disbanded. I felt really crummy because I had grown to like the group. They gave me a sense of belonging, and I felt that I was contributing to something special. Then I was given a chance to be in the existing Learning Community. I jumped at the chance. To me, here was a new road to travel, a new challenge to conquer.

My sophomore year started. I had found a program that actually gave students the freedom to help design their own studies. Here, I could follow my interests while achieving the education I needed in order to succeed. I wanted to learn more about the world and understand why things were so bad in El Salvador and so "good" in the U.S. I developed my study contract, researched areas of personal interest, and shared my ideas with the class.

Some of the things that I learned through my research were disturbing to me. My former country was involved in a bitter class war, one that involved the whole region of Central America. It was a war of the rich versus the poor, the "haves" versus the "have-nots." The rich, it turned out, were a very small minority of the country. They owned most of the land, directed the economy, and controlled the Army. When peasants tried to organize, they were imprisoned, relocated, or killed. Right wing death squads, funded by the rich, kidnapped intellectuals, teachers, and political activists. They intimidated or killed them and massacred entire villages. Even priests and nuns were assassinated. A most disturbing fact, to me, was that the people in power were funded by the U.S. government in its attempt to stop what was branded a Communist threat. My idealized road to U.S. citizenship took a rocky turn at this point.

I added my new research data to the old information that I had been taught in schools. The history lessons that I had learned in nine years of U.S. schools had not taught me about Central America, at least not what I had learned studying on my own for a few weeks. The official texts and courses of study appeared to be careful not to embarrass or offend the government. The texts were careful not to expose the foreign policy of its own government. I guess my teachers either didn't know what had happened or were protecting us from losing faith in the system and its officials.

Researching further, I learned that the period of my life in El Salvador—which seemed like an eternity to me—was a mere blink of the eye in the history of persecution and brutalization of native peoples in the Americas. One evening Gary attended a talk at a local bookstore by Victor Perera, a Guatemalan-born writer and journalist. Gary loaned me Perera's book, which traced the four cycles of conquest of Mayan people in Central America. The book described how the early conquerors took our resources, how the colonialists took our land, how the missionaries repressed and destroy our religion traditions, and how, in present time, the imperialists are stripping and destroying our environment. I had experienced first hand some of what Perera was writing about.

But my immediate challenge was to find some way to share my interests and studies with the rest of my class. Each week in our Community Meeting we planned the next three weeks and took responsibility to make presentations, facilitate discussions, contact local speakers, and organize field trips. Small sub-groups were responsible for implementing the larger group's objectives. My sub-group's objective was to understand how social systems affect the people of the world. Our task was to set up several activities through which the group could work toward their goal.

One of the activities was proposed by Erika, who had come to the US from Mexico. She wanted to conduct a seminar on *Proposition 187*, a state-wide ballot initiative that would prevent non-citizens from using the state supported schools and hospitals. She wanted to describe the volunteer work that she was doing with an organization that opposed the measure. Also, she wanted to conduct a debate on all the propositions that were coming up for a vote in our state in November.

I was surprised at the directions our group took these ideas. The discussions we had were different from those in my other classes. People opened up; they were really sincere. The day that Erika tried to explain Prop 187 and why she was opposed to it, Jeremy interrupted her presentation and said, "Well, I don't see why we should let *those people* into our country." His voice hung on "those people," emphasizing the distance he probably felt from migrants. Then he added, "They just use our schools and hospitals; they also get social security benefits when they don't even pay taxes."

My sister Wendy was pissed. She tried to speak through her anger and tears: "*Those people* you are talking about are people like me! My parents had to leave our country so we wouldn't get killed; and my dad has worked almost every day that he's been here."

"Yeh, well, illegal immigrants get Social Security, and it's breaking our system," countered Todd.

"No, non-citizens don't get Social Security," answered Erika, "and we do pay taxes! I work over thirty hours a week, and a lot of my money is taken for taxes." The discussion went on for about an hour before we took a break. It left a cloud of bad feelings hanging over the group.

We spent most of the next days processing our discussion. In the end, we agreed that, in the future, we needed to do a lot better job of researching our facts. Also, we needed to listen to one another and respect each person's point-of-view.

Wendy explained her frustration, "My family went through a lot—largely because the U.S. government supported the wealthy class in El Salvador." She continued, "We saw soldiers carrying new guns and wearing new boots, all provided by the U.S. We saw caravans of tanks and Grand Cherokee jeeps (we even saw the president of our country in one) that were used against our people. They, too, were supplied by the U.S. We had nothing. We came here for a new start, becoming legal residents through the Amnesty Act, and now, we've become the object of white America's intolerance toward Latinos."

The next day, Jeremy, who had been her chief antagonizer, brought up our discussion again, wanting to settle something with Wendy. He said, "I discussed the topic of immigration with my parents last night. My grand-father, who is living with us now, reminded me of my Jewish background and his flight from Nazi Germany to escape persecution. I'm sorry, Wendy."

I think we learned more about mutual respect from the discussion than we learned about immigration. Our group had grown close, but our behavior was still influenced by a lifetime of deeply-seated reaction patterns. I learned that it isn't easy to convince another person of my viewpoint just because I have lived it. I also saw how ugly things can be when people feel that their own quality of life is threatened. The road to the truth, I realized, is a long, hard road and needs to be lived with tolerance, understanding, *and* patience. Every time I tried to convince others, I was forced to grow inside, too. It seemed that every issue appeared in a new light as I saw it from other people's view, too.

The challenge, I realized, was to look for the value in each point-of-view from the perspective of a global citizen. That would be a worthwhile road to travel in the years ahead. For the immediate future, our group was learning valuable lessons to guide us in our discussions and in the way we related to each other.

When Erika shared her work as a political volunteer, we began with a simple presentation which turned into an unplanned class debate. We found ourselves embroiled in a full-fledged interpersonal, trying to unsnarl the hurt and angry feelings and misunderstandings that erupted in our group. Then, we set time aside to make sure that everyone had resolved their emotional issues; it was important to understand what was fueling our disagreements. Finally, we explored ways to conduct better discussions in the future.

In the end, we agreed that, while the issue of immigration was complex, our group's health was more important than winning or losing. So we decided to study the issue in more depth. We didn't want to avoid issues; we wanted to become better informed; we wanted to understand each other; and we wanted to understand the world. This decision opened the way for richer activities. Exploring cultural diversity became one of the themes that our group developed for the semester.

Some of our students were interested in learning more about the American Indians and how their lands were taken and their culture destroyed by the immigration of Europeans. Wendy, Alma, and I wanted to know more about the indigenous people of Central America, especially the Mayas from whom we are descended. The economist in our group decided to research the financial motivation for colonization of the Western Hemisphere. Our government specialists looked at civil law and ways in which whole territories and civilizations in the New World were traded about by the European nations. Some students were much more interested in contemporary political events and issues; they studied U.S. foreign policy in Central America and how it has evolved over the past forty years. Some studied the effects of foreign policies on domestic issues, like immigration. Some wished to read novels or poetry that brought eras and issues to life.

It became a very exciting adventure, with each person finding some way to share with the group. One student suggested that we each share our heritage; we ended up having a lunch at which everyone shared foods that represented their cultures. We shared places where we had found our favorite resources. We went to the public library and book stores together. Joe brought back a schedule of authors speaking at a local bookstore. We *surfed the web* and found data on almost any topic. We watched films: *The Mission, Romero, El Norte*. We hosted speakers from local development agencies. In addition to becoming informed, we were invited to get involved. Students facilitated discussions and gave presentations. We had more debates. After our first debate on immigration, we researched our positions more carefully and often chose to argue the opposing view. Words like *colonialism, imperialism, neo-colonialism, tyranny*, and *sovereignty* took on new meaning. Our whole class gave a technology demonstration at a teacher inservice using the curriculum that we had created.

I got to facilitate the playing of an immigration game for the class that I had learned from International Development Exchange (IDEX), a non-government development agency with which we were working. IDEX is a sustainable, global organization that matches First World donors to Third World projects. A few weeks earlier they had invited me to accompany their staff to Los Angeles to help make a presentation to the California Teachers of Social Studies annual conference. I accepted the invitation. After my presentation, I got to go to other presentations. That's when I participated in the *Immigration Workshop* for the first time and met the people who developed the game. They provided me with all the materials that I would need to run the game and encouraged me to conduct it for our class.

The class jumped at the chance to role play; and they met the challenge to think critically. The appealing thing about the game is that it offers policy positions in which there is no predetermined right or wrong choice. Participants are, however, asked to describe their underlying principles, and consider the ramifications of their positions. I asked the students to choose one of the following position statements about their country: 1) We should adopt a policy of open borders and let any citizen of the world enter and leave our country at will; 2) We should establish and enforce a fair quota of immigrants entering the country each year; 3) We should set up a quota for highly trained professionals and permit them to immigrate to this country only when we need them; 4) We should suspend all immigration and restrict residence in this country to current legal citizens. Then students formed small groups consistent with their position statements, discussed their positions, and presented to the larger group.

Later in the year our school sponsored a Multicultural Week. Janna, Adrienne, and I were invited to run the simulation for other classes. Our experience in working with The Learning Community gave us confidence and helped make our presentation more effective. Before Learning Community, there was one obstacle that held me back, and that was myself. I was not confident that I could work independently, that I could be my own teacher. Now I have done it. I have become more open to ideas, and my awareness of global issues has grown. Learning in such a unique way has made me want to become a better student for myself.

In past school experiences, I looked for understanding, but didn't receive it. Sometimes I felt as if school was just rushing by like a train that wouldn't stop to pick anybody up, and never slowed down. I felt left behind, and I struggled to get on the train, but I couldn't. I felt that, even if I was a passenger on the train, I would have little control of the route or pace.

In the Learning Community, I feel that everyone is on board and looking out at the world from the train. We are all on task because we all are willing to work together. That is the difference between being understood and being told or forced to do something. I don't feel pushed or rushed in the group. I learn things better when they are studied as a whole rather than being broken up into disciplines. Lessons stay with me, and I remember what I learn because I am active in the process. I enjoy learning. I can be a leader in The Learning Community. I am a person with a voice, and I can be understood for being myself. Now I am conductor of my train, and I am off to visit the world, wherever I wish to go.

As our school year progressed, the group had many more opportunities to develop group studies. We became more effective and learned to explore very controversial subjects with a spirit of inquiry. In fact, the *spirit of inquiry* became the focus for us. We enjoyed each other, and we enjoyed learning from each other. To me, that's what community is all about. At this point of my life, the road I had chosen was no longer simply leading to a safe refuge for my family or leading to the "American Dream" or even leading to some place. Rather, I had found access to a higher road which places real value on liberty and justice for its travelers all along the way and which has a high tolerance for truth. My road becomes our road; it can be shared by everyone on the planet; it is paved with *the spirit of inquiry*. On our road, we are all equal citizens of the world.

Passage Six:
Caring For the Earth

Protecting the Birds in the Nest

Kristie

When I was little, my mom ran a day-care center. In the spring she often took all her little kids to Lake Lagunita at Stanford University to see the Monarch Butterflies. My best friend, Adrienne, and I always tagged along. As our little band of curious kids walked around the lake, we found hundreds of caterpillars on the milkweed that surrounded the lake. Mom let us take a few caterpillars home at the end of our stay. Back home, we watched, with great anticipation, for the caterpillars to metamorphose into their chrysalis form and hatch into elegant butterflies.

After the butterflies emerged, we knew that it would takes about two hours for their wings to dry before they could fly away. I took special care of one of the newly hatched butterflies, which I adopted. I blew on its wings and swished it through the air to help it dry out. Then, I took it outside in the sunlight. Finally its wings became dry and strong so it could take flight. It left my hand, rose above me, and made two graceful circles. Then it swooped down and landed right on the tip of my nose. It was in no hurry; it just sat there resting. My mother ran into the house and got her camera. She returned and snapped my picture. Then the butterfly flew away. Mom always insisted that it was the butterfly's way of saying thanks.

I loved butterflies, but my real fascination was with birds. It was a solo activity, much different from playing horses or climbing trees with Adrienne. I spent hours watching birds as they ate, preened, built nests, and darted in and out of the trees and bushes. They seemed to come in all sizes and colors, with peculiar habits that distinguished them from one another. I wondered if they ever slept.

One day I was exploring around my neighbor's bushes. I was shocked to find a bird nest that had fallen on the ground; it was moving. I looked inside and discovered three tiny baby birds inside. I picked up the nest and ran home, careful not to disturb the little babies. I showed my discovery to my mother. She called a family friend who was familiar with Wildlife Rescue, a humane group that cares for wild animals that are injured or separated from their mothers. Our friend took the birds to the shelter where trained volunteers nursed the little birds and, when they were able to take care of themselves, released them. I was fascinated that people could raise birds and safely release them back to nature. I wanted to be a nurse to the little birds, too. It wasn't long before I took the *Basic Care* class at Wildlife Rescue. When I graduated, I became a volunteer. I was ready!

Early in the summer, I spotted a fledgling bird in my neighbor's yard. It was a towhee, a small non-descript bird that is usually seen foraging for food on the ground under bushes. It was just learning to fly and hadn't developed a fear of humans yet. So I crawled into the bushes, held my hand out to the bird, and let it perch on my outstretched fingers. The mother bird squawked at me. That got my neighbor's attention, and she squawked at me, too. I still got to hold the bird for a few precious seconds, before I had to go, dodging an angry mother bird as I left the bushes.

I checked on my fledgling friend every day before my neighbor arrived home from work. One day I saw a cat pounce on the little bird. I ran as fast as I could, screaming as loudly as I could, and chased the cat away. I was furious. When I knelt down to pick up the bird, my heart almost stopped. Its feathers were wet, it was trembling, and scared. Then I saw blood on its body and feared for its life. I took the little guy home and called the shelter. I was determined to save my little friend.

I was required to register the bird at Wildlife Rescue before I could get antibiotics for the bird. I administered the medicine and food with a small syringe. I had to open its little beak and squirt the liquid into its mouth, making sure that he didn't choke. He acted as though I was his mother.

The next step in the recovery of my patient was to get it a companion so it wouldn't imprint on me. Wildlife Rescue supplied me with a baby cowbird for that purpose. Someone had brought it to the shelter after it had fallen out of its nest. I nursed them both for about a month. After the initial excitement, I settled into the enormous task of mothering at only nine years old. I had to make sure that I fed them every hour during the day. My mom helped me, but I did most of the feedings.

After my part was finished, I took them to an aviary where they could move more freely and get used to life in the wild. This was the last stage of recovery, before being released. Each different species of birds required a different type of care, even a different type of aviary, so people in our community offered special locations to cater to different bird species. Wildlife Rescue coordinated a network of recovery aviaries around the community for this purpose.

Because towhees feed on the ground, they are easy targets for cat attacks. Once I found a towhee that had escaped from a cat, but sustained a broken wing in the process. I had to learn a tough lesson. If a bird is not releasable, the Wildlife Rescue has to put it out of its misery. The method is swift: the bird is placed in a container filled with CO_2; the bird just lies down and dies peacefully. Peaceful or not, killing anything was almost beyond my comprehension.

I had to adapt quickly—my feelings and the larger conceptual order of things had to come into balance. I found out that part of the care for an injured bird is to determine if it could ultimately survive in nature. Of course, as a little girl, I wanted to keep all of the birds alive as pets, but that wasn't permissible. It isn't legal to keep wild birds as pets, and it isn't ethical either. The towhee would never be tame so it wouldn't lead a normal life as a pet. I knew the rationale, but I wanted to keep it anyway. I had to turn my little bird with the broken wing over to Wildlife Rescue for disposal. It was a hard reality for me to accept.

I really don't know where my love of birds began. I was connecting with nature, to be sure, but my obsession with birds was more than that; it was my passion. When I went to Disneyland at an early age and saw the Tiki Birds, my passion was fanned even more. Mine was not like one of those childhood fantasies that disappears; it has stayed with me.

The elementary school I attended, Peninsula School in Menlo Park, California, had a wooded campus which I explored a lot. When I was seven, two of my classmates and I used to walk around the school and look under rocks to find creepy, crawly things. I couldn't imagine that happening anywhere except Peninsula. On one of these expeditions, we found a dead robin. We wondered what we could do with it. I got the idea to stuff it so it would look like it did when it was alive. My friends liked that idea, so we went to our science teacher for advice. Our teacher had taken a course on creating study skins for scientific research, so she was a good resource. It was a long way from a taxidermy mount, but we didn't know the difference at our young age.

We had an activities hour each day in which we could work with clay, weave, do art projects, work with wood, or work on a project of our choice. Rachel and I spent the next two weeks of activity hours preparing and stuffing the bird. Each day we did a little more work and then put the skin back in the refrigerator in preparation for the next day. It didn't look much like a bird when it was done. The skin had started to decompose and lots of its feathers had fallen out. But we were proud of our work. Rachel and I took turns caring for it at our houses after we finished our work. Peninsula encouraged our interests. I enjoyed science and made good use of the opportunities provided by the school to dissect a shark, a fetal pig, and a frog. Still, I enjoyed stuffing birds most.

Working with the robin sparked my interest in taxidermy—the science of stuffing and mounting animals. While Rachel went on to other interests, I took on taxidermy with a passion. It wasn't long before I was experimenting with wire supports to make my mounts stand erect. A local nature reserve hired me to mount birds that had died on their property. My mother insisted that I get formal training if I was going do mounts for others. She found a local professional taxidermist who was tickled to take on a young, enthusiastic apprentice. He showed me the proper techniques. In turn, I got him interested in doing free projects for local nature centers—it gave him a community outlet for his talents and a break from mounting heads for trophy hunters.

Somehow the penguin caretakers at the San Francisco Zoo got my name and hired me for a project. Aggressive sea gulls were eating most of the penguins' food at the zoo. This made it an expensive operation, given all the antibiotics and nutritional additives that penguins required. My job was to take a dead sea gull and stuff it to look dead. Gulls make a distress cry when they see a dead or injured gull. The warning cry causes them to fly away. It worked!

The zoo's newsletter reported the problem. It quoted the zoo keeper as crediting a local twelve-year-old girl for the solution. Then, I began getting calls from local elementary schools requesting me to make presentations. The teachers wanted someone close to their students' ages to stimulate interest in science. I took my egg collection, my nests, study skins, and diagrams into the classrooms. Word spread and I started getting similar calls from other elementary schools, scouts, and nature clubs. My collection grew; I added an owl skull. The owl has a bone plate that supports its eye; it almost looks like a pair of binoculars and gives the owl a panoramic view. The children were intrigued. At first, the children swarmed me with their questions, especially second graders. I had to learn to have them hold their questions until I was finished with my formal presentation. During this period, I was making ten dollars an hour mounting local birds for the Environmental Volunteers, a local docent training program.

One of my favorite nature spots was only a few blocks from my home. It was a ninety acre sanctuary on which St. Patrick's Catholic Seminary was located. The church used the building as a study retreat in which to train priests and nuns; I used the sanctuary to hone my skills as an amateur ornithologist. I remember going there as a child with my brother and our golden retriever; the grass was so tall I couldn't see over it. Years later as I walked home from Peninsula School, I would walk through the seminary grounds each day. The majority of my life-list of birds came from these walks—Goshawks, Dusky Flycatchers, Vireos, Hermit Warblers, Screech Owls, Red-Tailed Hawks, and Kestrels. Sometimes I would sit quietly and write in my journal.

I am sitting under the shade of a giant oak. The morning sky is beautiful. I breathe in the crisp, clear spring air. Above me is a nest of bluebirds. I've been watching the nest since the babies were small. Now, they are almost grown. I hear a sharp twittering. The mother bluebird has just kicked the baby out of the nest! It flutters back, confused.

She pecks at him to force him out again. How terrible! I sympathize with him. One day, you just get kicked out of your warm nest where you've been raised and nurtured. Your parents decide you're old enough and boom!, you're kicked out. Then I think about my own home situation and the stupid fights I have with my parents—curfews and such. Maybe it's not so bad.

The little blue bird flutters back into my brook of gentle thoughts; he lands on a branch of a tree just under the rising sun. In this serene setting, he peacefully preens his feathers. "Peacefully preens his feathers?!" I think, as my thoughts awaken to what has just happened. "Peaceful?" I wonder, after the little guy has just been kicked out? Maybe that's the difference between wildlife and people. Birds see life and death in simple ways we cannot comprehend. Never will you see a bird grieve or be swarmed with emotions. The baby bird is on his own now—free.

Today is not much different than yesterday for the bluebird, only a slight change in instincts. Follow the force saying "search for food on your own" instead of "gape for momma bird." Just another day in the life of the species.

I am flying over the brook of gentle thoughts. It quietly laughs at me as it trickles down and parts the trees. A breeze blows across my face. Everything is so beautiful from here. A great view of the valley. I am flying. Wind rushes by. I just believe in me. The view is so good. I can see my family from here. Everything is beautiful from here.

I remember how horrified I was the first time I watched the soil being tilled at the seminary. Nature has its own way of managing dry grasses, but tiller blades make deep cuts into the ground, unearthing and killing gopher snakes. I witnessed whole populations of reptiles being eradicated. They were vital links in the food chain.

Still, the seminary grounds were my place to escape the hustle and bustle of the city. There, I could find peace. It was my place to commune with nature, to watch the sun set, and watch the animals in their natural ecosystem. The observations that I made contributed to my knowledge base. I felt the land; it was part of me. One day I was sitting under an oak, the sun was setting, my journal was at my side. I was startled by the loud sound of a Peregrine Falcon diving straight toward the ground just a few feet behind me. Its folded body sliced the air—it was practicing its *stoop* for prey. The falcon was so close to me that, when I turned to look, I could clearly see the colors of its wings, body, and tail. The black markings on its face stood out like a mask. It dropped straight down and recovered without hitting the ground; then it resumed flight. I was amazed that it could change directions so abruptly and fly so close to the tree tops.

When the seminary was damaged by the 1989 Loma Prieta earthquake, the church decided to sell some of its land to pay for the repairs. To cover the cost, they chose to sell most of their land, which was prime real estate for developers. Local environmental groups were priced out of the bidding by rich investors, who purchased the land. It was the beginning of the end for my place of solace.

The proposed development called for a gated community with large, expensive homes. The project required city council approval of the use permit, building permits, and zoning changes. Big developers, big business, and big money, largely from outside our community, supported the subdivision. The neighbors, who didn't want more population density, more traffic and less open space, opposed it and persisted in attending city council meetings, collecting signatures, and drafting an initiative. A major battle ensued.

Supporters and protesters took their positions at the city council meetings held to discuss the proposal. I was surprised that only two or three people spoke in favor of the subdivision, though. I knew most of the people who argued against the project. Even though more people lined up on our side of the issue, the city council seemed to be favoring development. Our cause was beginning to look like a lost cause. I had one idea to fight the development; it was a long shot, but it seemed reasonable to me.

I knew that the Peregrine Falcon, which I had seen on the seminary grounds, was endangered; and I knew that endangered species habitat was protected by law. I had met only one other person, an older man and an amateur ornithologist, who had seen the falcon. I talked to him and he agreed to support my observation at the council meeting.

I requested an official Environmental Impact Report and read it carefully. I was surprised to find that it didn't fully represent the bird populations, or even list all the present species. I had counted more than ninety different species of birds on the seminary grounds, the report listed fewer than twenty. In parts of the report, some species were mentioned twice—once by names in current usage and a second time by names that were no longer used by the scientific community. To this thirteen-year-old, the Environmental Impact Report seemed to be a pretty sloppy piece of reporting.

A final meeting was called to hear the community's concerns before the subdivision was to be approved. One council member, a neighbor of mine, had asked me before the proceedings, "Why are all these people talking and wasting their time at our meetings? You know that they don't have a chance to win this issue." He may have been right about the eventual outcome, but I wasn't ready to concede. I was disgusted at his cavalier attitude. He dismissed the environmental position without even trying to understand it. I signed up to make a presentation at the next meeting.

My family and friends went to the meeting and so did members of local environmental groups. Again, I was surprised that so few people advocated for approval. Once again, I didn't recognize them as people I had seen in Menlo Park. I knew many of the people who spoke against it. One protester cited studies in which sick people healed faster in a serene environment. He asserted that our community needed more open space for the health of its people, and that it had already reached a critical population density.

The city council members looked annoyed. It was discouraging for me to watch them. One was tapping his pencil, some leafed through papers, and others seemed bored with the environmentalist's pleas. The council members didn't even look up at some of the presenters.

I heard my name called; my stomach erupted like a flock of partridges. I looked around. The place looked like a courtroom; official flags stood at the front of the room; council members, mostly men in business suits, sat stuffy in a semicircle of padded wooden chairs, as if ready to circle the wagons in case of attack. My nervousness evaporated—the experience was pure passion for me. I walked to the podium and delivered my speech. I really put myself into it; I said what I had to say. My friend Rebecca told me later that when I asserted, "Endangered species habitat is protected by law!" councilmen came out of their slumber and took notice. I pointed out that the Environmental Impact Report was inadequate, sloppily researched, and had made no mention of the Peregrine Falcons. I went on to address the specific points of the report. As I turned to take my seat, I got a big roar of applause. I couldn't help but smile as I walked back to my seat.

Shortly after I delivered my plea, there was an intermission. A man in a business suit came over to me and asked, "Where can I see your falcons? On what part of the grounds do they live?" I was thrilled that someone else was interested in my passion, but something made me suspicious of this stranger. I asked him who he was. His reply was that he was a nature lover and that he "favored the land." He said that he lived in Atherton, a wealthy community nearby, and saw hawks in his yard all the time.

I gave him a vague description of the location. I was naive, also. After the intermission, I noted that he sat with the group of developers and their lawyers favoring the subdivision. Then, I learned that he was the primary developer! My stomach sunk to my feet. I felt that I may have betrayed my Peregrine friends. This event left me very distrustful of well-dressed strangers. After the meeting, I went back to him and told him other places to look for the birds. I wanted to throw him off, but the act seemed futile; the damage was done. I worried for several days.

On the bright side, my speech caused a delay in the approval. Because of the potential for damaging endangered species habitat, the city was required to hire a wildlife biologist to investigate my assertion. I got to accompany him to the seminary. I took him to the site where I often saw Peregrines. We didn't see any, but the biologist said that, in this case, an actual sighting was not critical to his report. When we parted, I asked for his address and requested a copy of the Environmental Impact Report when it was completed. He expressed surprise at my request and commented on my maturity. I felt good about how I was conducting myself.

The biologist's report to the City Council concluded that the seminary grounds were not considered to be a critical habitat to the Peregrine population; it was not the birds' breeding grounds. Since the birds were migratory, the seminary was simply their wintering grounds; they could move elsewhere. As I thought about the dwindling habitat in my community, "elsewhere" seemed pretty remote.

The City Council released their final draft, stating that they had addressed the public's concerns and concluded that there was not sufficient reason to block the proposed subdivision. They approved the land use and building permits and allowed the entire project to go through as proposed.

Months later, the former seminary grounds were transformed by heavy equipment. A giant wall was constructed to conceal the million-dollar homes that were being built. The wall isolated the houses from our larger community while creating a rift in the middle of our community. Today two controlled gates keep the general public from intruding on a spider web of private cul de sacs with manicured lawns that exist inside. The native oaks and native grasses are gone forever. The dead trees, which were wonderful niches for Acorn Woodpecker and other critters that live in tree cavities, or hawks that sit on big open branches looking for prey are gone forever also. The next little crop of girls like me will be relegated to cement and asphalt playgrounds to help them prepare their minds for the inevitable onslaught of so called *civilization*.

I visited the site during construction. I took my binoculars with me in hopes of catching one last glimpse of any bird-life that might remain. A guard approached and asked brusquely, "What are you doing with that camera? Are you here to take pictures?"

"No," I told him. "These are my binoculars, I am just looking for birds." He put my name on a report form and said that if my business was done, I should leave. I thought to myself that this guard must have gotten his education in a pretty sterile concrete-and-asphalt environment.

One small field is left near the renovated St. Patrick's Seminary; there are no trees on it; but it's like money-in-the-bank to the church. At one million dollars per acre, they can rest well. I don't rest so well as I pass the new development—all I can see is a high, colored wall. The two gates leading into the development each have twenty-four-hour-a-day guards. I will never see inside those walls again; I really don't want to; the sight would tear up my heart.

I needed to move on. Education, it is said, is the key to success. But education comes in many forms—some more inspirational than others. I had the good fortune to attend a school that did inspire, one that embraced children and made them a part of the school. It was a place where the excitement of learning something new was a bright and joyous experience. Learning didn't simply appear in books. It sprung from the everyday life experiences of the students and teachers who share them.

I am a Peninsula School graduate. It is hard to explain what that means to someone who has only experienced a traditional school. Individuality, love, compassion, and a joyful environment can produce amazing results. I cherish every memory I have of Peninsula. It brought out my creativity and uniqueness. It gave me an opportunity to work with others; it gave me a chance to have some of my needs and ideas carried out. When I am loved and accepted, my energies expand. In a stressful learning environment, all my energy is absorbed in fighting routine and in coping with stress. In a safe home-base, I can expand my energies into interests, community work, and creativity. Good schools could work miracles for society.

Peninsula school really helped nurture my passion for the outdoors. It's the kind of school where you can squish your toes in the mud, or stuff birds—if you are me. Teachers become buddies, not unapproachable authorities. My science teacher—my close friend—encouraged my passion. I appreciate just how much the staff nurtured my creativity. *They inspired me and then got out of the way—so I could shine*. Unfortunately, the school only went to the eighth grade.

I braced myself for the public schools and went to Menlo-Atherton High School, about a mile from my house. "MA" was a school similar to most other high schools in the area. I don't really remember my freshman year. I never really opened myself up to thinking. I just passed the school year away sitting in class passively doing homework. It was a non-event in my life. Sophomore year was my *poser era*, a period in which I created an image of something that I am not. It was also my more rebellious year; I was bored and wanted some action. Near the start of the year, I decided to see what I would feel like if I got stoned. At lunch, I'd hang out with the parking-lot people, who talked about dumb things like how many beers they could chug. I put on my I-don't-give-a-shit act so that I would fit into the crowd. When we weren't in class, we were smoking dope on a dirt trail near the baseball diamond.

I was just a follower that year. I was following something that wasn't me. I was getting nowhere, like a rudderless ship. I still longed for Peninsula. My wish was to have one more Peninsula day sharing love with all my old classmates. I had to accept that it was gone and I'd never get it back. This wasn't easy for me. The combination of my loss and the lack of fulfillment at MA fueled my frustration and anger.

In March, I tried LSD. A whole new world opened up. In April, I took it three times in six days. A new world of *bullshit* opened up, I realized. I only took it one other time; then I stopped. By the time my sophomore year was almost over, I realized I wasn't pursuing myself; I wanted that to change; I knew I wanted to be me. That's when I stopped smoking dope.

I started dressing in my own way; I started acting like myself, instead of like the person I thought others wanted me to be. I rearranged my personality. I no longer wanted to be isolated from people: I wanted true friends; and I wanted self-identity. My mom sensed my need. She didn't want me to go back to MA for my junior year. That became a certainty the day she picked me up at school and a car load of kids drove by shooting guns in the air.

We began our search for another school. A family friend recommended The Learning Community. He had close ties with families whose children had had positive experiences there. Also, we knew that Paki, a former Peninsula School student, was returning for his second year there. We checked it out, and I applied. I felt like a fifteen-year-old lost waif when Gary interviewed me that summer; fortunately, we liked each other. I longed for the peer relationship that I had experienced with teachers at Peninsula, and thought I could have this kind of relationship with Gary. Besides, sitting in a desk for fifty minutes while some teacher filled me with useless information didn't appeal to me. Working with a group of twenty-five kids to develop our studies together did appeal to me. I enrolled for the fall term.

It wasn't until after our three-day Venture Retreat, three weeks into the year, that I felt secure with the group. Bonding with the group and seeing how much we could accomplish when we were all working together really helped me. After that I began to understand Paki's intensity to live up to his commitments. He would come by my house early in the morning to give me a ride to school. I would say, "Hey, Paki, we could leave later and still get there on time." But Paki always insisted on leaving early. After Venture, I realized that it really wasn't much of a sacrifice for me to be on time and keep my commitments. I started to feel better about myself. Then later on, when I started driving my own car, I left early as a matter of course. If I happened to get to school fifteen minutes early, I could just hang out in the room and get to know Janna or Joe better. Still, it took the first semester to acclimate. I just took things in.

I loved the way Learning Community functioned. Here was an approach to education that seemed to erase the separation between school and life. It created a classroom bond that made me feel at home. It felt like a progression beyond what I had at Peninsula. Gary helped us understand how our personalities functioned, and worked with us to fine-tune our group dynamics. He helped us see that we had many dimensions within our being—physical, emotional, intellectual, societal, environmental, and mystical. He said that a basic challenge in life is to understand ourselves as a whole person. I remember thinking about how confused I got when I only viewed myself through a small window. I longed to be able to see myself in a larger sense.

My experience wasn't perfect. Work started piling up and I felt overwhelmed. I had to create and fulfill my study contract. Resistance set in, I began to feel hesitant about The Learning Community—afraid I'd been brainwashed or something. Although some of my optimism subsided, a new feeling of knowing myself didn't. My hesitancy toward the program went away as I discovered that I was being challenged to move beyond the familiar and away from past, limited definitions of myself.

Since my enrollment in The Learning Community, I have created a path for myself, and have discovered more of who I am. When I got lazy and wanted to stop, The Learning Community kept me going. When I caught myself slipping off the path into self-denial, I fought back. I couldn't turn my back on what was being shown to me. The Learning Community taught me about myself, about education, and self motivation. The psychology seminars opened doors into what I hide inside and defend against. I learned that human beings are similar in their resistance, and I learned ways to overcome my resistance. And I got perspective; Gary told me something that I will never forget: "There is a time in the lives of most people when they think they know everything. But as time passes and they find out there is more, they come to the realization that the more they know, the more they find they don't know."

There was so much I didn't know about myself, although I was making some pretty important discoveries. I learned that *no one is alone*. I don't have to be. I can choose to make myself feel alone. From the honesty and openness I have seen in each person during Venture and the "interpersonals" and from my own experiences, I know that I am not alone. We are all in this world together, and we can help each other.

I've learned how to make a commitment, and I realize that *anything can be achieved if one commits*. There have been some things in my life that fell through because of my lack of commitment. In The Learning Community, I've seen commitment really make a difference.

I learned that *I will succeed if I persist*. At the beginning of the year when I was feeling stressed, I didn't know what to think. I almost let myself fall again. I realized that we all have our ups and downs, and, if we persist, eventually things will come around. I saw this happen during our Venture Retreat and during SIMSOC (the Simulated Society experience we shared). When all seemed lost, our group hung together and pulled through.

Also, I learned that *education is the key*. At MA, there were times I thought high school was the end of the world. It wasn't. I've come to like school so much more since I've taken charge of my education. I've been able to do things that benefit me, things that are worthwhile. Books are one way of learning, but there are so many more ways to learn, ways that aren't available in regular school. Life is learning: we learn from mistakes; we learn from being together. Most importantly, we learn through experience by working together.

It wasn't until the second year that I really started to take initiative and to help facilitate the group's discussions. It was a real bonus to be joined by my childhood friend Adrienne—my butterfly partner. We could share the experience and she was a great motivator. I started to blossom as I applied myself. I took the next step, to make school the dream that I knew it could be. I wanted to help make something beautiful and I knew that if I applied myself and our group applied itself, we could succeed.

As the year progressed, many things stood out. Our group made a decision to open up our schedule one day every two weeks and engage in community service work. The time gave me an opportunity to get back into the elementary classroom again.

I wanted to share important lessons that I had learned during the year: that in order for the world and its environment not to crumble and die, we all have to make commitments and modify our lifestyles to achieve the world we want. For the first few weeks, I was invited to teach a third-grade class. I took some of my taxidermy and bird skulls and taught them about different beaks and feeding habits. I wanted to teach more. I let kids know that they could make a difference—locally and globally. They could set up bird baths and feeders to help local bird populations. They could get their families to recycle and to be environmentally responsible to help the global environment.

The light of enthusiasm is bright and alive in kids. On our nature walks, the kids always gathered around me with bright eyes, personal stories and continual questions. Their lives seeped into me and gave me more power to want to help our world. Helping the environment is the most important issue facing our world today. We can make a difference with the help of dedicated and compassionate children.

One of the speakers that Learning Community invited into our classroom came from Magic, a local human-ecology collective. He invited us to help a group of volunteers plant and care for oak trees in the local foothills each week. He explained that the foothills had been grazed for over one hundred years. Each spring, the young acorn sprouts were eaten by the cows. Consequently, the foothills have old growth oak stands, but no new growth. This condition, if it continued unchecked, would result in the elimination of the oak forest. Another impact on the ecosystem, was the one-way flow of nutrients. As a cows eat the grasses, some of the energy is burned for the animal to live and some of it is added to their weight of the animal. When the animal is slaughtered for food, the ecosystem is depleted by the amount of energy burned. The cow is not an efficient food system.

I enjoyed the physical exertion of planting and caring for trees and welcomed learning about the environment. Also, I profited greatly from my interactions with the Magic community. Here were seven people living in one house, with one seldom-used car and a bountiful garden. They were fully dedicated to a sustainable lifestyle. They took so little from the community, and they gave back so much: planting trees, leading workshops, and making presentations to the city council on vital issues. Each week they opened their home to the community, inviting people to eat food, to dance, and to share in the joy of living. I was inspired.

Magic also shared its resources. One of the members of the Magic community gave me a book about biodiversity entitled *Shattering: Food, Politics, and Genetic Diversity*, by Cary Fowler and Pat Monney. The book focused on the food system, especially on the plants that we raise to eat. Years ago, the range of foods grown by farmers was so broad that no single pest could devastate the food supply that we humans depend on for survival. There was enough diversity for species to be able to survive in a changing environment. Today, that broad diversity has dwindled down into a narrow line of specially-bred vegetables, with many of their diverse cousins long gone. I realized that lack of diversity poses a real threat to the human species.

A friend at Magic taught me about Seed Saver Exchange, an organization that grows and maintains a broad selection of grain, herb, and flower seeds for distribution on the planet. They are dedicated to helping maintain plant diversity at a time when global agricultural practices have moved toward single high-yield crops. I began to learn about environmentalism on a large scale.

Also, I began to understand how our day-to-day living, our lifestyle, affects the environment. I was beginning to extend my interest in saving birds to saving the planet. What our lifestyle supports or how it impacts the Earth is vitally important. I applied the understanding of commitment that I learned in the Learning Community to the larger issues of lifestyle and sustainability. We *can* do something to help save the environment; our contribution is real and immediate. We can conserve in the way we live our lives—day-to-day. We are the true *birds in the nest* and the nest is our environment. We can educate ourselves to clean up our own nest and put it back in order.

I took my new awareness back to the classroom. I offered to teach an SIS—a student initiated seminar—on biodiversity and sustainability. I started by sharing my knowledge about birds. I brought in a live American Kestrel, who sat through my presentation eyeing the class, and a stuffed owl. The Learning Community students huddled around my skull collection and wanted to touch everything. In some ways their enthusiasm was like that of the second-grade class; They asked questions like "Did you stuff that owl by yourself?" I felt supported. They showed a deeper respect for what I did. I didn't even mind their calling me *bird woman*. As with my second graders, I had to remember to defer all their bird questions until my presentation was complete.

Next, I shared a paper, which I had received when I attended a summer institute sponsored by the School For Field Studies in Montana. The paper summarized the *Caring For the Earth* conference on sustainable development held in Switzerland. I shared the key point made by scientists at the conference that genetic diversity is essential for species survival in the ecosystem and for planetary evolution.

I wanted the class to know that the ecosystem is vulnerable to sudden environmental changes, that we have lost many varieties of food crops, and that we are causing changes much more rapidly than organisms can adapt to them. If we do not take care to preserve biodiversity, we create an unhealthy system. We have made and are making such a system on the planet now. It is a system with narrow and specialized features, one in which sudden environmental change can result in the disastrous loss of a crucial species. We as humans depend on this highly specialized system and we are vulnerable, especially in our single species food crops.

I told my classmates how I have begun to look at my total lifestyle. I gave concrete examples of how my daily choices contribute to the development of a viable environment: riding my bicycle instead of driving in cars, eating organically-grown food free of pesticides, putting on a sweater when I am cold instead of turning on the heat, and staying physically active in nature to maintain direct contact with the Earth. I explained how the passion that I feel now has grown from a childhood desire to protect and nurture the wild birds to include larger environmental concerns. I have developed a new lifestyle and a new consciousness.

I have become aware of the impact of my life on the planet. This awareness, along with my example, helps me to educate others so that they can be aware of their impact on the planet. We must each do our share in caring for the Earth. Our lives and the lives of generations to come depend on us. We must each become protectors of the birds *and* the nest.

Passage Seven:
Embracing the Collective Spirit

Harmonizing the Voices in the Choir

Angel

My mom tells me that when I was a very small baby I had two undeniable attributes: I had a strong voice and I was stubbornly outspoken. She recalls that hours after I was born, while I was lying in my hospital bassinet, I raised my head and looked around as if to survey my new world. She was concerned when she saw me. She asked the doctor, "What is my baby doing raising her head when she is only one day old?" He told her not to worry, but mom knew from the beginning that she was going to have her hands full with me.

Shortly after my mother brought me home from the hospital, she took me to the doctor's office for my shots. She said that after the nurse stuck the needle in my thigh, I raised my leg straight up to the sky and let out a scream that could be heard around the block. Mom figured that I was making my protest to all concerned. It was as if to say, "Don't you know that you are hurting me?!" I really don't know what it meant—but I still don't like shots.

At three-and-one-half months, I was crawling, and at six months I was standing, but I only did these things when my mom was around. Mom told others of my feats, but they dismissed her claims as those of an overly-proud mother. This all changed when a family friend walked into my bedroom one day and caught me—a seven month old child—climbing up the partially-opened drawers of a dresser so that I could jump off the dresser onto the bed. They didn't think my mom was crazy after that observation. I'm not sure what they thought of me, though.

Mom did her best to contain and direct my energies, but she said that I had a mind of my own and that she couldn't watch me every minute of the day. Sometimes she would wake up in the night to check on me and find me sitting up in my crib trying to get out. She said that I would persist in whatever I tried, no matter what it took—I had a determined body and I had a determined mind.

One night after a hard day's work of preparing for our family's holiday barbecue, my mother was awakened by noises in the house. When she opened her eyes she saw a light coming from the kitchen and she could hear metallic sounds, like pots and pans crashing together. She was frightened and tried to wake up my father. "Roosevelt, wake up! Somebody's in the kitchen." she whispered.

My father rolled over, tried to calm her with a kiss, and then whispered back to her, "It's just your imagination, Betty, now go back to sleep."

My mother wasn't easily dissuaded by my father's excuse to go back to sleep. She rose from her bed and crept into my bedroom to see that I was all right. All she could find in my crib were pillows and covers—but no Angel. She thought, "Oh my God, Angel's been kidnapped! And the burglars must be taking everything in the kitchen, too." So she grabbed one of my toys for a weapon and tiptoed her way to the kitchen. She peeked around the corner. There, much to her surprise, she found me all bundled up and sitting under a stool. I was holding a big slab of ribs and munching on them like it was the thing to do. She couldn't help but laugh out loud. At eleven months old, I was dwarfed by the huge chunk of meat in my hands—and mouth. She said that I was so engrossed in my feast that I didn't even look up when she came into the room. It was such an unbelievable sight that she ran and got my father so he could see me holding a rack of freshly cooked ribs, barbecue sauce all over my face, and my mouth stuffed full of juicy meat.

I was fascinated by things that moved. At fourteen months, I borrowed my brother JoJo's skates. A neighbor called my mom to report that I was skating down the sidewalk. Mom had to work overtime to keep up with me. It wasn't long, though, before my abundance of energy was channeled into my true calling and number one passion in life, singing.

Singing is my gift from God and is a major priority at such a young age. Most of my singing was inspired at local churches where my mother played the piano for Sunday services and other church functions. I went to choir practice and to church with my mom almost from the time that I was born. It became second nature for me to sing along. I memorized the words of the songs and hymns that the choir sang—even at age two and three—and it wasn't long before I was actually singing before the church congregation.

Not only did I accept singing into my heart at a young age, but I accepted God into my heart as well. And from that point, singing and the church became one for me. I was surrounded by spiritual people—my mother, my aunts and uncles, and my grandparents. My grandfather was the pastor of a church. I sang in the churches so much that people recognized me as soon as I entered. Some parishioners even greeted me with a smile and a nickname. They called me "Mahalia Jackson Number Two."

Of course, I still hadn't completely reckoned with my childish independence. Most of the time when I was asked to bless the church with a solo, I would jump at the request. But sometimes I didn't feel like singing. On one such occasion, I stated plainly, "I don't want to sing today."

One of the other parishioners rose to my support and shouted out, "If she doesn't want to sing today, she doesn't have to." This seemed perfectly acceptable to the pastor and the congregation, but it wasn't acceptable to my parents.

When we got home that evening, my mother had a serious talk with me. In her calm, motherly way she said, "Angel, listen, I know that there are times that you don't feel like singing. Honey, that's okay when you are singing for yourself. But when you are singing for the Lord, sometimes you have to give when you don't want to. You need to share the beautiful gift that the Lord gave you with others. You never know when someone in the congregation needs to have his or her heart touched. You never know if this will be your last time to touch others. This is what God would want you to do." With tears in her eyes, she embraced me, gave me a hug, and kissed me good night. I never refused to sing in church again.

My talent and reputation as a gospel singer grew faster than I did. At age two, I was invited to sing on the Wilson Brother's gospel music program held at the Zion Missionary Baptist Church in East Palo Alto. Unity Church was like my second home, though. I sang in the choir and was involved in all the children's activities. I was encouraged and inspired by members of the church. I was respected because I was willing to do God's will, and, with that focus, I always gained their support.

Still, I was challenged to harmonize my outgoing, sometimes aggressive, energy with my natural gift for song and my deeper calling for celebrating the spirit that I felt so strongly when I was in church. I was a normal child in many ways. Like so many of the other children that I grew up with, I loved to run and play at the park and I loved to watch Sesame Street. But I was also encouraged in ways that most children are not.

When I was five years old, my uncle, who is a minister, invited my mother and me to his congregation in Detroit. He wanted me to be the headliner in a gospel concert. Posters placed around the Detroit neighborhood proclaimed that "the miracle baby" would perform in concert on Sunday. The banners and the tickets read, "*ANGELITA BURGESS IN CONCERT.*" The master of ceremonies introduced me as the "Little Angel." I was a small child with a big voice, singing to several hundred people—and I was as nervous as I could be.

As I began to sing, silence spread over the audience. All that could be heard was the quiet sound of my voice singing the words of a traditional hymn that had been sung during slavery:

> *Precious Lord, take my hand,*
> *Lead me on, let me stand,*
> *I am tired, I am weak, I am worn.*

As I sang, I could see faces light up in the audience. I could feel their warmth; hands began to raise as if gravity had been turned upward. People's lips began to move; I could hear their voices praising the Lord. I was inspired and my voice grew strong.

> *Through the storm, through the night,*
> *Lead me on, to the light,*
> *Take my hand precious Lord, lead me home.*

As my first song ended, I was greeted with "Amen!" "Yes Lord!" and "Hallelujah!" There was always a great spirit of worship in the wonderful Baptist churches that I grew up in. They certainly loved to hear the praises of the Lord in song, and everybody found a way to involve themselves in the service. Call and response was part of every sermon and every song.

Singing in Detroit was a remarkable experience for me. I even earned $400 dollars for singing. Getting paid was strange though, because I always regarded my singing of the Lord's music as *giving testimony* rather than *entertaining people*. Getting paid for giving testimony didn't make sense, even to this five-year-old.

I was deeply moved by the spirit of the church. When I was six, my Aunt Ruby died. My mother was going to the funeral, but she hadn't intended to take me. I wanted to go the funeral—I wanted to be involved in everything in the church, even in a service for someone who had died. When my mom denied my request, I told her, in pleading words, "I know about death, mom. Please let me go to the funeral!" She relented. Two years later, I sang *Walk Around Heaven All Day* for our neighbor Ralph's funeral.

As my singing matured, my opportunities to sing became more frequent. I got to sing with the *Soul Stirrers*, a group from my community. My independent energies and my musical talents continued to blend, but not without difficulties. I still had more energy than I knew what to do with. To channel my physical exuberance, my mom enrolled me in a ballet class. In class all the other little girls were doing the teacher's dance routines. Not me; I was running, diving, and doing flips and somersaults. I had fun on the mats. My antics drove my teacher crazy and distracted the other little girls. So mom took me out of ballet and enrolled me in gymnastics.

In the first grade, I enrolled in the South Bay Christian School. I remember being proud of the little red dress that I was wearing on the first day of school. I was excited by the idea of school, but I had a hard time conforming to the regimentation of school. It seemed to me that most of the little kids had their mischievous streaks, like I did, but that the other little kids would tell on me when I did something to them. I didn't know the *game*, so it didn't occur to me to tell on them. Consequently, I was seen as the perpetrator. When I finally figured out the game, I added a twist of my own. I bit myself and blamed it on a little boy that had been bothering me the most; he got in trouble. At the end of the year, because of my behavior, the school didn't invite me back for the next grade. It worked out okay for us though. By then my mother was a single parent. She worked hard to support me and the $300 tuition for school was a hardship. So she enrolled me in a public school.

I attended Theurerkauf School for grades two through four. It was an exciting time for me socially; I made lots of friends. Then on to Crittenden School for fifth through eighth grades. I was always active, sometimes more than what the teacher wanted, but I learned to apply much of my energy to running, all kinds of sports, and dancing. Singing, of course, still ranked as my favorite activity. I began to write poetry and music. Some of my teachers asked me if they could keep my writings. I felt special and was inspired to write even more.

When I was nine, mom thought that I would benefit from formal music training, so she enrolled me in Chuck's Academy of Music. The instructors helped me to train and control my voice. During this period, I received a *Good Neighbor Award* and sang at the Martin Luther King, Jr. Holiday Breakfast sponsored by the city of San Jose. The mayor commended the award winners and thanked me after my song.

My singing in the church continued. I recall my mom telling friends that, "Angel filled the church with the Holy Spirit." I would get embarrassed when she praised me too much. I was both embarrassed and humbled when she would say to her friends, "I've never known a person so young that has such talent and, at the same time, knows and loves the Lord."

Our family had a deep faith and trust in God; we learned through my grandmother and the church. We built our lives around the church and we trusted in God to guide us in our everyday life so we could endure. Life wasn't easy for us; mom worked hard to support our family. God brought us through so much and we depended on him for everything.

When I was ten, I participated in a singing competition. I sang the spiritual, *I'm Looking for a Miracle!* During my song, a woman got the Holy Ghost. She jumped up and she shouted. She praised God right there; she wasn't self-conscious or intimidated. She was in God's hands because, after the Holy Spirit took control, she had no control over her body and mind.

Afterwards, the lady said she hadn't gone to church that morning; instead she had a premonition to come to the competition. She told me that I had helped her touch God. I didn't win the contest, but I felt that I had served a greater purpose. Some of the people in attendance told me that I would win in a much bigger way another day. I felt that I had already had a winning day. My mom says that the Lord must have sent us to the competition to inspire that lady's heart.

I didn't always sing alone. I was also part of the church choir. We had so many big, strong voices in the choir that I had to shout my message to be heard in the harmony of so many voices. When our choir rose up and sang the praises, I felt as if we were touched by the Holy Spirit. I loved to harmonize with the choir and the congregation; it was as if we sang with one voice. I experienced one level of personal harmony when I sang my solos, but I experienced quite another level of harmony when I sang with the choir.

When I was eleven-years-old, some members of our church started a street ministry to move the drugs out of our community. On weekends we went into the neighborhoods where homeless people, drug addicts, and drug pushers hang out. I sang songs and our group delivered the word to the people. Some of the hard-core people would leave. Those that stayed could listen to the word of God without having to be bothered by people who weren't interested.

When I got to high school, I became involved in activities that nourished me and my schoolmates. I helped start a gospel choir with Tamika and some of the other girls at school. We called our group the *Voices of Light*. I joined the *Los Altos Steppers*, a precision drill team—with soul. I also enrolled in The Learning Community; I needed room to be myself and I wanted to help make school more exciting. I knew some of the people that had been in the program, and they all talked about having grown personally and having built a community together. I wanted to do something special in high school and I needed more flexibility in my life.

I was trying to balance a blossoming professional singing career with my school activities and my singing in the church choir. I had made some appearances in concert as a featured vocalist with rapper M. C. Hammer and I got to record a popular song and a gospel song on his CD. I even got to perform on television with him on the *Arsenio Hall Show* and *Soul Train*. It looked as if I would be doing more of this. Yet, I still had to deal with high school and with my personal life.

One of the studies that particularly interested me in The Learning Community was *Psychological Systems*. It was a course that our teacher had developed over the years that explored models of personality and spirituality. It wasn't at all as I thought it would be—rats running around in mazes, men in white coats looking inside people's heads, or crazy people in an asylum. It was much more personal. I discovered why I do the things I do, what I could do to get along better with others, and how my view of the world compared with others.

I didn't need help from school to understand my purpose on the Earth—that came from my church, but I did need help to understand why and how I continually got off track. My ever-present question was, "Why don't I always do the things that I really know I should do?" I was at home with the spiritual world that I knew inside me—the Spirit is perfect. But I was not as at home with all my day-to-day actions. Life was not so perfect. Sometimes, I felt like that *little Angel,* still enrolled in ballet class, tumbling on the mat while the rest of the class did *pirouettes*. I wanted to understand myself in the world so that I could be the Christian that I wanted to be.

At the beginning of my first year in The Learning Community, I watched carefully to make sure that the teachings in psychology didn't conflict with my faith. I noticed that my classmates grew and changed in ways that they wanted to change and that they did not change their faith. As I began to get involved in the seminars, I began to change as well. My mother was pleased as my attitude and behavior became more positive.

I learned many things about myself. I learned that events in my past, some of which I had even forgotten, influenced the way I responded to people and circumstances. As I thought back to important events in my life, I wrote about them in my journal, and discussed them in the group, I noticed that I began to act more from awareness and less from reaction. I listened to other student's stories as well. I was deeply touched by Greg as he shared his story; he was so open and honest.

Sometimes, I attempted to rescue others when they were being confronted for not being responsible—I came to realize that it was my way of protecting myself from being responsible. There were times when I wanted to leap in and stop my peers when they confronted Tamika about being late. I had my own problems with being on time.

I found that I engaged in "flight" or "fight" reactions when I was confronted—more often in fight—and tried to manipulate people by shear force and by being right. I got reactive when I got pinned down by the group or caught in a game. I didn't agree with Jeremy's seemingly racist attitude, but I squirmed when he got pinned down.

I developed ways of keeping others at bay or protecting myself from the truth about myself. I discovered that I rationalized my behaviors or denied my responsibility. It was easier to see these defenses in others—I noticed them most in Shawn. Many times I didn't own up to my behaviors until well after the event had passed.

I learned lots of things that helped me understand myself better. I learned that I was an extroverted-sensation-thinking-judging type. My tendencies were different from those of others, yet all of us acted out our types. It was reassuring to know that my uniqueness was okay.

I saw how I could shift from being a "critical parent" to being an "angry, rebellious child" during the heat of conflict with my mother. I experimented with more effective approaches in dealing with her; it was easier to resolve things when I wasn't so reactive. I learned how I hide from my own abilities and, at times, settle for less than the best for myself. Certainly this was true in my contracted studies. Also, I discovered that I could understand myself better by watching how my body reacts to stress. Sometimes I assumed a defensive posture as Shawn did when he got upset.

As my fellow students and I became more self-aware, we learned how to be more effective with one another. We confronted our peers when they were acting like victims and asked them to be responsible, to take charge, and not to go into self-pity. We challenged each other to be aware of the truth of our actions instead of projecting, reacting, or denying. We urged each other to use "I" messages and to be honest about our feelings. We learned theories about group dynamics and applied them to our group. We insisted that group conflicts be resolved—no matter how long they took. And, we always brought disputes back to the principle of gaining personal power by taking responsibility for oneself and one's actions.

In the final analysis, I learned that, with all my new awareness of who I am, it is up to me to take charge of my life and make it work. The more I learned and became aware and the more I engaged in constructive confrontations, the more my daily behavior changed. A more healthy, socially-conscious Angel began to appear. Oh, I wasn't perfect. I had relapses; sometimes I got mad or pulled back from the group. But I could tell that a subtle change was taking place in my personality. I felt freer; I felt more responsible; I felt more power in my daily life. It was as if a heavy hood was slowly being lifted off my head and my vision was getting clearer.

I found myself going home and teaching my family and friends some of the lessons that we were learning. It was interesting to see our lessons move from personal awareness to personal power to personal responsibility. I liked the way we progressed from personal harmony to group harmony and I was curious to see how this could be taken to the next level. We discussed how moral reasoning progresses naturally from "What can I get for myself?" to "What is my duty to others?" to "What can we agree to do together?" I was especially intrigued by the final question: "What principles guide your behavior in helping to create a better world?" Second semester, this question became the guiding question for our decision making. I felt that I was in the process of cleaning and sharpening the focus of my spiritual lens so that I could be a better person in the world. I was developing a healthier anchor in the material world and I looked forward to applying this new clarity to my spiritual life.

As our group's awareness, ability to resolve conflict, and decision-making improved, we made ready for taking action in the world. The nature of our Psychological Systems course changed as well. We had been concerned with understanding personality and group dynamics to this point. Now we were about to shift our emphasis to understanding spirituality. We had had a glimpse of the Plains Indians' spiritual view of life at the beginning of the year when we had studied *Seven Arrows* by Hyemeyohsts Storm, a Native American author. During the second semester, we explored the philosophies of the major religions of the world. During that time we were introduced, briefly, to some of the major spiritual systems of the east: Buddhism, Hinduism, Taoism, Sufism, and Yoga.

Gary told us that his approach in Psychological Systems was "an invitation to join others on the path of seeking wisdom." He acknowledged that we each had our own personal set of beliefs. He suggested that by studying other major belief systems in the world, we might gain insights into the mind of the human species. His invitation was for us to attempt to understand other paths for their insight into human nature. That way, in understanding the spirit of each belief system, we might get some insight into the fundamental nature of human beings.

I was confused by all of this so I spoke up, "I don't need to discover the truth through these systems; I already know it through my faith."

Gary replied, "Your personal views are valid for you, Angel. I respect you for the strength of your religious beliefs. My goal in the seminar is to help you understand and appreciate the attempts that other cultures around the world have made to bring their view of the world into daily life. As we understand spiritual practices and systems that humans have built over the centuries, we may gain further understanding into the nature of human beings."

Privately I remained confused. I looked at different sides of my life. I had always been taught by my church that there is only one truth. My family and my culture confirmed and reinforced the teachings of the church. I grew up as a cute little girl with a beautiful voice. The voice, my mother told me, was given to me by God to do his work. I wondered if I would still be doing God's work if I worked with people that didn't believe what I believe. I wondered also how they could be doing God's work if they didn't believe what I believe.

At this point Jenny spoke up. "Angel, I had some of your same concerns last year when we studied spiritual systems. I've been a Mormon since I was eight and I think that I have become a better Mormon from studying other religions." I let my concerns go for the time being, but I watched cautiously and tried to be objective.

Gary went on to offer a metaphor to help us understand his approach:

> *Imagine a large, hollow lead sphere in the middle of the room that contains the truth about the universe. Imagine that human beings across the centuries have probed this sphere to understand its hidden message. The exploration for truth is like drilling a hole into the sphere. A person looking into that hole gains one perspective to the truth hidden within. As this "truth" is spoken or written, it represents a point of view of the larger, whole truth. Others, who might*

journey to that view point, see the truth from the point of view of that entry point.

As other entry points are established and as other points of view are elaborated upon, additional insights about the ultimate truth are revealed. Over time, as more entries are made known, a greater sense of the mystery of the sphere is revealed. Some points of view seem contradictory and some versions of the truth are limited by their language or interpretation. In the end, each seeker of the truth is left to interpret his or her version of the truth, to accept a given truth, to simply conclude that we will never have enough information to really know, or to conclude that the sphere contains nothing.

Each of us in the class has his or her own spiritual perspective. You live in a predominantly Judeo-Christian culture although some of you may be Buddhist, Hindu, Muslim, or a member of some other world religion. Some of you may still be seeking a religious affiliation. Some of you may be agnostic, believing that we, as mere mortals, just don't know the deeper secrets of the universe. Some of you may be atheists who simply don't believe in a god. It is a personal choice how you wish to function in the world—and in this seminar.

Whether you are a person who has committed to a religious path or you are a person who has no interest in committing to a path, you can view our class experience as simply a way to understand other cultures and beliefs—view it as an intellectual exercise. A person who is looking for a spiritual path will only get a brief overview from our study—you will have to look elsewhere if you wish to look deeper into any of these systems. A person who has an inner spiritual life but no wish to commit to an established religion might use this experience to get some clarity into the nature of spirituality. The way you use the information you obtain from this class is entirely up to you.

In the first Psychological Systems seminar of the new semester, we were given an opportunity to share our spiritual cosmologies. We shared our core beliefs about life and death and analyzed how those beliefs affect the way we live. Each person took a few minutes to share how he or she saw the world; everyone else listened and learned. I was amazed at the diversity in our group. Some students described mainstream Christian beliefs—Baptist, Presbyterian, Lutheran, Methodist, Episcopalian, and Catholic. Others described beliefs with which I was unfamiliar—Unitarian and Sikhism. Our discussion was an eye-opener for most of us. Some didn't know the difference between Protestants and Catholic; others didn't know that both religions were Christian. Still others didn't know that Judaism was based on the Old Testament and provided a common base to both Protestants and Catholics.

A big surprise for me was hearing some of our students—some of them good students and leaders—say that they were agnostics or atheists. My biggest surprise was hearing Adrienne say that she didn't believe in an external source of God, that spirit existed in everyone and everything. She said for her, "It doesn't matter whether there is a God or not. In either case, I would live a life guided by my principles. I would still love and be kind to everyone." She added, "Being spiritual is noticing that the birds are singing and the sun is shining." I couldn't understand how Adrienne, of all people in the class, could be so committed, so hard working, and so positive without getting her motivation from God.

When it was my time to share, I spoke proudly of my faith. I described it in detail—how those that were good would go to heaven on Judgment Day and how those who were sinners would have to live for seven years on the Earth with one last chance to redeem themselves. I made it clear that you had to be *saved* in order to go to Heaven and that all those who were not saved and who hadn't accepted Jesus as their savior would go to Hell on Judgment Day. This assertion set off an intense discussion in our classroom.

Jeremy asked if I believed that he, an agnostic, would go to Hell. I said, "Yes, but you could convert and be saved." Others asked what I thought about their religions. I repeated my belief that they wouldn't get into Heaven—they didn't like to hear that I would be saved and they wouldn't.

Janna asserted, "There are many paths to God. It doesn't matter which path you chose. What's important is how you live your life." Others said that they agreed.

I held my ground. "There is only one way," I said. It wasn't a popular comment among many of our group. Some even got upset; it was like the temperature of the room rose by ten degrees.

Gary stepped in before it got out of hand. He reminded us, "This process was meant to give people an opportunity to share their beliefs. Each person is entitled to have his or her beliefs, and one's religion is not subject to debate!" He asked us to respect each other's differences and learn from one another. He said that we needed to find common ground so that we could work together.

Then he recited a poem, *Abou Ben Adhem* by James Henry Leigh Hunt, that he had learned in the sixth grade. It was about a man who was awakened in the middle of the night by an angel who was writing in a golden book. When he asked her what she was writing, the angel replied, "the names of those who love the Lord." He asked her if his name was in the book, and she said that it was not. "Write me then, as one who loves his fellow men," Abou said. The next night, the angel reappeared and showed Abou the book, and "Lo! Ben Adhem's name led all the rest."

We went on with the seminar. The discussion that I had initiated cast a certain discord that reverberated through the group. I knew clearly that I was right in my beliefs and yet, given the resentment that my remarks left, I felt confused how to continue. How was our group ever going to achieve a common purpose when we had such diverse beliefs? How could we go beyond our differences and unite behind common principles to create larger goals? I just didn't know how.

I thought back over some of the things that we had learned. I wanted to take personal responsibility for my action. How was I helping to create this feeling of discord in our group? I thought back over my life. There have been many times when I've been in complete harmony with a group and times when I haven't felt completely in tune. As I sat there, I felt a tightness in the pit of my stomach—something wasn't right. I tried to understand what principles were involved in this issue. I knew that my beliefs were not negotiable, but then no one was asking me to give up my beliefs. The real antagonism was coming from people feeling that they were wrong.

My church taught me that I was always a voice of God, but it also taught me that, if a person wasn't interested in my message, I needed to respect his or her wishes. The hard thing for me to admit was that I may have helped create tension in the group by invalidating some of the other student's beliefs without even realizing it. I had a hard time sorting out being right and doing wrong at the same time. It took a long time for me to put it all together.

As the year progressed, I realized that the group needed to find a way to work together. I wanted to find a way to make my contribution. We needed to find a way to get everyone to work toward some common good. On one hand, we had to be faithful to our personal beliefs and values and, on the other hand, we had to find ways to unite our group behind some common principles. To do this we needed to accept our differences and be tolerant of each other's beliefs, then find ways to work together. I wasn't sure how this was going to happen. I needed more insight.

I thought back to critical times in my life when I had needed to pull myself together. Usually when things weren't working out for me, it was because my body, my emotions, and my mind were each calling me in a different direction. I had to listen for a deeper voice inside me to lead a harmony of all my voices. When I could go within, my actions became harmonious. It was no different from harmonizing with my church choir. When each member of the choir lent his or her voice to a higher purpose, our choir made beautiful music.

I thought back to earlier in the school year. Some of my inner voices had been calling me in different directions. I noticed that these voices were starting to change. One of these voices used to be quick to judge people—

now I am training that voice to be more accepting. Another inner voice stated a feeling; I attached myself to that voice. I was unable to separate my personal feelings from the real teaching of my faith. As the year has progressed, I have been getting better at telling the difference. Now, I am better able to detach myself from the personal feeling and express the real voice.

My new perspective has helped me to voice to myself that "we are all God's children." I realize how much better that is than my saying, "I have the answer." It helps me to see and it encourages me to look more deeply into my religion. I am able to relate to my peers with a clearer voice. I am able to approach people with a positive, non-offending voice. My message has become more harmonious now. People are willing to listen to me when I am willing to harmonize with them.

I realize that each member of The Learning Community has strong values and principles. Together we have a higher purpose—everyone is in agreement that we want to work together to make a difference in the world. Like the voices in the choir, each of our voices is unique. We can raise our unique voices in harmony to make a difference. I realize that it is the difference in the voices that creates the harmony and it is the purpose in the collective voices that creates the melody. I want to join the other voices in our group and create more harmony in the world, the kind that brings joy and happiness into other people's lives.

Passage Eight:
Being in Service

Discovering the Essence of Learning

Janna

My first school experience was in a private school. My parents enrolled me in a Montessori school so that I could get a good start in life. Classes were small and only extended to the third grade. I felt close to my classmates and enjoyed the combination of freedom and structure that the school provided. When I transferred into the local public school in the fourth grade, I adjusted well, but things were obviously not the same. I wasn't very aware of the contrast then, but looking back with the perspective that I have now, I can see that the two schools had completely different views on education.

At the Montessori school, there was some structure, although it was minimal. The amount of free time exceeded the amount of teacher-controlled time. Students were required to learn basics skills, such as reading and writing, but a major portion of the learning was left to the students' initiative. It seemed to me that their philosophy was to teach the basics and let the children develop independently by following their own interests. As students, we thrived on creative activities—we were constantly designing projects, organizing field trips, or putting on plays. We learned responsibility and real-life skills as we organized and carried out our activities.

I was only eight when I entered the public schools. I adapted easily to my new environment. I learned to do what I was told so I sat dutifully at my desk most of the day. It didn't seem to really faze me at the time. The basic philosophy behind the public school seemed to be that the a student is like a blank slate and doesn't really have much to offer to the process of learning. The belief seemed to be that a young mind needs to be filled with information in preparation for the "real world." Participation in that world was to be delayed until later. I had some inspirational teachers who made me think that there might be something more to education, but most of my experiences in public schools reinforced my view that the student's role was meant to be passive.

The atmosphere at the Montessori provided a better learning environment for me. It wasn't perfect, sometimes kids made fun of each other and weren't very supportive, but we were given the freedom to explore, to communicate, and to work things out socially and intellectually. When I got to the public schools, I was far ahead of my classmates because of the accelerated pace at Montessori. I enjoyed having that edge, but I lost it after a few years. I think, perhaps, that I adapted too well to the public school environment. I was so eager to please that I hardly noticed the change and quickly got used to being told what to learn. I always got good grades and was considered one of the "smart" kids.

My fifth-grade teacher kept a list of the five "smartest" students on the wall of our classroom. I was always on the list, but my best friend was always right above me on the list. Even now, I don't understand what purpose the list served. If it was some sort of motivator, even for a few students, wouldn't it be motivating us in the wrong way? Isn't the purpose of school to learn, not just to get good grades?

Junior high wasn't any better for me. I continued to get good grades and tried to please my teachers, but something didn't feel right to me. By the time I got to high school, I had grown pretty discouraged with the public school system. I didn't feel "seen" by the the system. I began to think more critically about my situation. Grades seemed arbitrary and lost their power of motivation for me. Teachers seemed to make mistakes, too, and didn't always know the answers. My life revolved around lectures and homework. I wondered why, if the process of regimentation and schooling was really working, our time was still being controlled as we got older.

Still, I realized that I, like most other high school students, was dependent on external forces for control. I lacked true self-discipline. I went to class every day and did my work to get good grades and approval from my parents and my teachers. But I wanted more from school and I wasn't sure how to get it. Things didn't get better. I developed a problem with tardiness. I was late to my first period class almost every day. I think it was my way of passively and secretly rebelling against a system in which I was beginning to doubt.

During my sophomore year, even though I continued to get on the honor roll, I thought seriously about quitting school and teaching myself at home.

I read the *Teenage Liberation Handbook* by Grace Llewellyn and was even more inspired to quit. My mind was pretty much made up that I would not return to school for my junior year; my parents supported this choice. And I probably would have left school if I hadn't heard about The Learning Community.

When I first heard about The Learning Community, I feared that it would not provide me the amount of freedom that I wanted with my studies. I was concerned, though, about the potential isolation I might experience in home schooling. As I found out more I realized that, although I would not have as much freedom as I wanted, The Learning Community would be a huge improvement over regular school. I also realized that I could become really close to a group of people my age. That had never happened to me before in the public schools and it would be very difficult to create as a home-schooler.

On the last day of my sophomore year, The Learning Community called a meeting for all the students who had enrolled for the coming year. I was annoyed at having a meeting on the last day of school. I didn't want to talk about school; I wanted to be free for the summer. But I decided to go in with an open mind. I walked into the room and watched as my future classmates filed in. We spent the entire meeting going over the commitments that we were asked to make when school started again. The commitments seemed like a good idea, but I didn't really take them very seriously. I had grown accustomed to "accepting" what went on in school; I treated this experience in the same manner.

I was pretty wary when Paki, a second-year student, first mentioned "choice points." He defined a "choice point" as a point in time when we still had an opportunity to affect the future. Gary helped explain it by saying, "If we really want to have power in our lives, we need to be accountable for who we are and what we do." He continued, "When we make a commitment and break it, we can learn from the experience. All we need to do is look back over the most immediate time frame and discover the point at which we consciously or unconsciously chose to break our word. Doing this will enable us to be more conscious the next time we are given such a choice. If we apply this principle consistently, we can begin to gain true power in our lives."

I didn't have a problem with the concept during the summer meeting, but when school actually started the next year, I saw choice-points as rather "point-less." If I was in danger of being late, I hurried to class to avoid having to sort out my choice with the class, not because I had agreed to be on time. If I thought that I was going to be late, I would plan out exactly what I was going to say. My words might not have had anything to do with my choice. More often, I used whatever excuse sounded good or seemed foolproof.

I'm not sure exactly when I realized the importance and the value of choice points. But as the weeks continued, I found that by being in the Learning Community I changed tremendously. One of my major changes was realizing the power of my own word. Knowing that my word actually meant something gave me more power in my life. I chose more consciously and was rarely tardy after coming to that realization.

Shortly after school started, our class went away to the mountains for a three-day retreat at a place called Venture. Our group response to the experiences at Venture completely amazed me. The closeness we created brought in an extra measure of trust and honesty that helped carry us through the school year.

The activity for the first night at Venture was something that we often referred back to as "meal planning." Everyone assembled in a big circle in the main meeting room. Our second-year students and our teacher were to be observers during this community-building process. They brought out all the bags of food for our three-day retreat. Gary gave a long talk about our purpose for the year and explained that we were to plan our meals "as a microcosm for the entire year." He said that we wouldn't be able to eat our dinner until all the second-year students and Gary agreed that we had completed our task.

Everyone started by attacking the problem in his or her own way. People were running around chaotically; some had to yell to be heard over the confusion. A block of cheese was thrown here, and a loaf of bread was thrown there, but we were getting very little accomplished. A half hour went by, then an hour. Finally, the food got sorted out in a semi-organized fashion. We had to get the observers to approve our plan, but when we asked if our task was completed, we got an unceremonious "no" from every single one of them.

We responded by developing more elaborate plans; these got turned down, too. Some students got discouraged and just sat around or slept, some got mad and argued with other people's ideas. We were up against what seemed at the time to be an enormous challenge and we didn't know what to do. It wasn't until about two o'clock in the morning that we finally figured out that planning the meals was not the real point of the exercise. Our challenge, it turned out, had little to do with what we would eat or who should cook.

The point was that we all needed to cooperate and pull our group together— without direction or help. Also, we needed to create a sense of community and a mutual respect that would guide our experience throughout the year. There were times that night when I wanted to cry, and a few people actually did. When we finally got the point of the exercise, I felt elated. So did everyone else. The lesson we learned could never have been taught. It had to be discovered. The experience brought everyone much closer together. We had established our basic trust and our own way of being together.

At last! A real learning experience in which everyone in the group drew from his or her own inner source of knowledge and found a way to communicate and build a group trust. Each of us had to go beyond our old ways of working together to obtain our goal. We truly discovered a way to work together. Our next step was to perfect our new skills.

Over the next two days, we learned to examine our behavior, give and receive feedback, and support one another. This was to be an ongoing process that was an essential part of our experience together. Our level of sharing and disclosure deepened with each new experience. I poured some of my feelings into my journal:

> *I can't believe this whole thing is making me so emotional. I don't even know what to write. I just want to break down and cry, but I can't. I feel so close to everyone now. People said completely personal things. I cried constantly. In the beginning, when Brenda, Paula, and Wendy were talking, I couldn't believe that more people didn't break into tears. When I see people I care about cry, I can't help but join them. I get so emotional so easily. I feel close to everyone now. So many times, I just wanted to get up and hug people, for them as well as for myself. I feel like we have all become much closer. I keep repeating that, but it is definitely something that bears repeating.*

In the weeks that followed, I made significant changes in my awareness and conduct because we took the time in class to hear and support each other. I wanted a close relationship with my peers, and, by opening our schedule to include human issues as well as academic pursuits, I was given a chance to become really close to a group of people my age. The bond among the students in The Learning Community is something that wouldn't be possible in mainstream classes the way they exist today. I gained a closer relationship with the twenty-five students in The Learning Community than I had made with any group in my entire life.

Another powerful experience that gave me greater confidence in myself and helped our group develop an even deeper bond of trust and teamwork was the Ropes Course. Our experience began with an exercise in which we had to fall backwards off a picnic bench into the arms of our peers:

> *"Spotters ready?" / "Ready!" / "Ready to fall?" / "Fall on!"*

These shouts rang in my ears as a gut-wrenching feeling entered my stomach. If I had known then the things that I would accomplish later on that day, my nervous feelings would have quadrupled immediately.

That day was one of the most physically and emotionally demanding days of the year—and certainly the scariest. As I watched one person after another fall from the picnic table into awaiting arms, I got more and more nervous. By the time it was my turn, I was scared to death. Despite my fear, I climbed up, squeezed my eyes shut, and let myself fall backwards. I was caught in a net of clasped arms. Relief flooded over me as I was lifted up and placed back on my feet. That was just the warm-up exercise. We spent the rest of the morning on a progression of events at ground level. We became more confident, built group trust, and learned to cooperate—and we had fun.

After lunch, having completed the low events, we moved on to the high events. The first of these was a tightrope about thirty feet in the air. We put on a belay harness, climbed the tree, positioned ourselves on the tightrope, and walked across it using only a rope tied to one of the trees for balance. Again, I watched the other people go, but I only got more and more scared. When Brenda panicked, I could no longer control my fear; I started crying. As I stood on the ground, looking up at that wire, I felt that I would never be able to do it. When it was my turn, I was still sniffling. Then I started to climb up the tree. I climbed, walked across the wire, and jumped. The belay rope caught my fall and I was lowered to the ground as if I were Peter Pan in a school play. I had completed the event before I had even realized what I had done. I was amazed. I felt liberated!

After I completed the exercise, I felt as if I could do anything, no matter how impossible it seemed at first. The entire day at the Ropes Course was exhilarating. I gained skills that I will use the rest of my life, skills that had little to do with climbing trees. I was gaining confidence in my ability to work through my fear and to complete whatever task I might try. Sometimes I look back at that day and think, "I was able to do *that* then, I can do *this* now." It was an experience that I will never forget. At the end of the day, I felt strong inside, connected to the group, and elated.

We developed positive group attitudes at Venture and at the Ropes Course that found their way into the daily workings of our group. When we encountered an emotional or intellectual challenge, we dealt with it directly and supported each other through it. We knew how to succeed.

I remember one day when Alma came to class very upset and said that she didn't feel connected to the group. It was uncharacteristic of her to bring personal issues to the group or to share her feelings with the group. She was like me in that way; I really didn't want to be the focus of a group "interpersonal." She started to cry; she spoke of random thoughts and feelings that she had stored up all year and had never mentioned. Most of our group members were caught by surprise at this sudden flood of emotion—but not me. Withholding feelings was all too familiar to me. Through her tears, Alma recounted a dream that she had had the night before. In the dream, she said, I had confronted her—without fear—for not really being involved in the group. When she said my name, I felt the same kind of terror that I had felt at the Ropes Course. "Am I going to have to be involved in an interpersonal?" I wondered. "Surely not," I thought. "Besides, I don't even know Alma very deeply."

Paki, Brenda, and Joanna consoled Alma, saying that they thought she seemed really involved with the group. Gary agreed that Alma seemed comfortable in the group, but he questioned whether "comfort" equaled "involved." As the group gave support to Alma and drew her out, she mentioned my name more than once. Apparently, I was a symbol for her of someone who was involved and assertive—a model that she could not live up to. Frankly, neither could I; assertiveness was not my strength.

Gary saw something in the group's dynamics that gave me more anxiety. He asked Alma and me if we were willing to explore the process together. We consented. We started by unraveling our thoughts and feelings about our involvement in the group and about our fear of bringing things up in the group. Gary noticed that neither of us spoke directly to one another or looked into one another's eye. He asked us if we were willing to stand up and experiment. I consented, hoping to end my part as soon as possible.

He asked us if we would explore the space that we had between us. We were on opposite sides of the circle; the space seemed like miles. As we probed the space between us by moving into the circle, the air took on the properties of thick glue. It was hard to move. Alma said her feet seemed stuck to the carpet. As we looked at each other and shared our feelings—mostly fear at this point—we began to move into the circle. The closer we got to each other, the harder it was to move or to speak. When we were a only step apart, we both froze momentarily. The moment seemed like an eternity.

It was clear to me that Alma wanted to reach out. I felt frozen, scared, and confused. Then Alma stepped forward; she was vulnerable and open. My arms extended outward, as if guided by instinct, and we hugged. The hug felt almost like the reunion of a long-lost mother and daughter (I am easily five inches taller than she). As we hugged, I felt tears streaming from my eyes. I could feel Alma's quiet tears expressed in her labored breathing. I felt other arms close around us as people from the circle came forward and joined us. Soon the entire group closed in around us. The room was aglow with twenty-five people encircled in a giant hug. One word best described the feeling in the room—love. Our whole group was open and involved; the sticky glue of fear was dissolved. From that day forward, I found it easier to open myself up to the group.

Throughout the semester, each of us gained greater awareness of ourselves and became more open to each other. Our group got closer and we learned to resolve conflicts and make decisions. The group goals that we made opened a window to the world, and, as our studies expanded, we started seeing how events in the world were interconnected. The most important shift of consciousness came when our group began to understand that we had the power to make changes in the world. As the first semester drew to an end, we were completing the activities that we had planned in our goal-setting process at the beginning of the year; we were ready for the next step.

Gary said that over the years some groups had chosen to create their second semester in the same manner as they had created their first semester and that others had not. It was our choice to make. He offered to take us through the goal-setting process again as one option. We decided to find our own way. We wanted to make the second semester more *project based* than the first semester had been.

We arrived at our mid-year point with a semester of enriching experiences, a group of finely-tuned students, and the freedom to create our new semester any way we liked. That opened many doors. We started by spending one day evaluating the previous semester and another in brainstorming what we might do second semester. The two activities actually blended as one. Our first semester had been a success, and certain project strands had emerged from our work together. Members of our group had already been trained to teach in elementary schools as Environmental Volunteers (EVs), and International Development Exchange (IDEX) had already helped us become aware of development issues in Third World countries. We made proposals for the second semester based on what we thought might be most productive, most beneficial, and most fun.

We debated and discussed which activities would be best for us. Our first semester's activities had taken us *into the world*. We had hiked at Jasper Ridge Biological Reserve, shared African drummer Samate's performance and cultural overview, and studied global events. Now we wanted *to get involved with the world*. Some people in the group wanted to do something that would make a difference in the local community. Some wanted to reach out and connect with people around the world. A few expressed the concern that we might just get too busy, be too task oriented, or become too fragmented as a group.

Our brainstorming produced five proposals: to fund a Third World development project, to continue to volunteer at local elementary schools, to plant demonstration gardens, to travel to Mexico, and to write a book. We spent an entire day discussing the time and energy required to complete each project. Each project had its own appeal, and it was hard to eliminate the favorite project of any particular group member. "How do we get past this one?" I thought. We had found a way to overcome almost every obstacle during the year, being creative and inclusive. Perhaps that approach would work now.

Adrienne came up with the magical solution. "Maybe we could find how these ideas are interrelated. Then we might be able to find a way to do them all." We were able to find many common threads in our proposed projects. We started by reviewing our first semester goals: *understanding nature, appreciating diversity, teaching children,* and *conserving the environment.* Our vision was to *build a strong community so we could explore and contribute to the world.* The five project proposals were consistent with our first semester goals and with our vision statement.

We could serve the local community by teaching at one of the neighboring elementary schools. We could serve the larger global community by helping to fund the project in Mexico that IDEX had introduced us to. We could learn and apply organic gardening principles at our own homes and compare our efforts to those of a Mexican community where people were learning about healthy living. In the midst of these projects, we could self-reflect as we collaborated on a book about our experiences.

The projects could be ongoing, such as with the writing project; periodic, as with the Environmental Volunteers project; seasonal, as with planting our garden; or concentrated, as with the Mexico trip. We had eighteen weeks in which to accomplish everything. That seemed like enough time.

Piecing together such a comprehensive plan was too inviting to pass up. After deliberating, we decided to do them all. We agreed to implement the five projects and began making plans for the new semester. Time permitting, we would intersperse other activities that supported our first-semester goals. Our basic plan was to

- *Support a Third World development project. Through a school partnership with the International Development Exchange (IDEX), we will raise $780.00 to support a nutrition and school-ecology project in Mexicali, Mexico.*

- *Teach environmental science to elementary-school students. Through a training program offered by the Environmental Volunteers, we will teach science-discovery units to elementary school children.*

- *Plant vegetable gardens. A group of us will enroll in organic gardening classes at Ecology Action and then teach the theory and methods to our class. The class will plant demonstration gardens at some students' homes.*

- *Take a field trip to Mexicali, Mexico to visit the Nutrition and Ecology Project. The class will take a six-day field trip to Mexicali to gain a greater understanding of our development efforts and of the Mexican culture.*

- *Write and publish a book on our educational experiences. We will write about our stages of learning and show how students of diverse backgrounds and abilities can learn to work together for the betterment of the world.*

Phases of the five projects overlapped and intertwined throughout the semester. We planned fund raisers to kick off the semester. We discussed many ideas on how to raise $780 for the Mexicali Farming Project. Adrienne brought a proposal to us from a professional acting group: We could sell tickets to their production of Shakespeare's *As You Like It,* and we could keep half the proceeds from our ticket sales.

Greg liked that idea. He pointed out that one of our group goals was to experience and express our creativity. He said that a partnership with the acting company was one way to fulfill our goal. As the idea caught on, Greg offered another suggestion. He proposed that we act out some scenes from another play, *Romeo and Juliet,* to give us more appreciation for the work of Shakespeare. He also said that we should all go to *As You Like It* with our parents as part of the fund raiser. It took less time to get everyone to agree to sell tickets than it took to get everyone to agree to read and act out a Shakespearean play.

In just two weeks, the group sold enough tickets to earn the money for the Farming Project. During that time Greg got us copies of *Romeo and Juliet.*

Our reading culminated in acting out the famous balcony scene on the football bleachers. Greg played Romeo and I played Juliet. I felt pretty strange hanging over the rail of the bleachers saying "Wherefore art thou, Romeo?" to Greg who was standing below. It must have played pretty well, though, because when we finished there was more applause than laughter.

The Nutrition and Ecology Project appealed to me. The project was designed to assist the people in a *colonia* (neighborhood) in Mexicali, a transient Mexican border community, to increase their understanding of and involvement in core community issues. The project seemed pretty simple: the community would be brought together at two elementary-school sites to plant gardens. The people (and the children at the schools) were to share the vegetables that were grown and were to receive lessons about nutrition and the environment. We worked with two organizations, IDEX and Los Niños, to carry out our part. IDEX (in San Francisco) connected us with the project. Los Niños (in San Diego) worked directly with the Mexicali population to set up the gardens and to teach the people. Our part was to fund the project and expand our knowledge.

Throughout the year, IDEX made enrichment presentations to our class. They conducted games to help us become more sensitive to people of other cultures, helped us understand the role of non-government organizations in Third World development, and facilitated role-playing exercises to help us understand the function of the World Bank in Third World countries. They also brought the project director of Los Niños from San Diego to visit our classroom and to help us understand the impact of our project on the people of Mexicali.

Another of our projects focused on local service. The connection that we established with the non-profit Environmental Volunteers during the first semester continued to thrive. The EVs train students as science instructors to teach in elementary schools. Fifteen of our students went through the five-day training. Then we were linked with adult volunteers who provided us with sets of lessons and teaching materials. The Learning Community sent teams of students to each of three schools—Monta Loma in Mountain

View, Hoover in Redwood City, and Beechwood in East Menlo Park—to teach one day every two weeks.

The remaining students in our group found other community service projects on which to work. Mitchie volunteered at the Veteran's Hospital; Shawn and Joe planted vegetables for the Hidden Villa kids project; Andy tutored at Peninsula School. Paki organized files for the Humane Education Network as well as teaching at Beechwood. Alma kept the books for a kid's soccer league.

Alma also taught at Hoover with Jenny, Paula, Victor, and me. Alma's situation was unique. She was giving back to the people who gave to her. She was born in Guatemala and had moved to Redwood City with her parents when she was eight years old. She spent four years at Hoover learning how to speak English; now she was teaching in the school. It was gratifying to see the delight on her face the day she reunited with her former ESL (English as a Second Language) teacher in the faculty room. I'm not sure who was most proud. They both just stood there and smiled at one another.

Hoover is located about fifteen miles from our school in a neighborhood with a large population of recent immigrants from Mexico. Although I hadn't worked with limited English speakers before, I felt comfortable because the children welcomed us with such great enthusiasm.

We were assigned to teach first and third graders. The science units provided by the EVs covered subjects ranging from fish to rocks to seeds to animal tracks. All the units had hands-on activities with ample opportunity for discovery. We even had the kids making paper. The teachers welcomed us into their classrooms and helped us feel comfortable. I did feel some frustration because the lessons were so structured and didn't emphasize enough of what students could do at home to help the environment.

The students enjoyed learning from people who were close to the ages of their older brothers and sisters. Looking back, I realize how good it was for the kids to learn from us. We were young enough to be able to relate to them. We could be friendly and make them laugh and keep their attention. And we could get serious and teach them simple scientific concepts or inspire them by our example. I felt special because the students always asked us when we were coming back.

I was particularly happy to be teamed up with Jenny. I wanted to teach in a school with a diverse ethnic population, but I was anxious about teaching so many kids who couldn't speak English. Reaching these kids was made easier by team teaching with Jenny. I was able to teach in English while she taught in Spanish. Teaching was a challenge for Jenny, too, since she hadn't learned science or ecology terms in her native language. She was not shy about asking the students for help with Spanish words. As the kids were called upon to help provide some of the vocabulary, they became more involved in the class and more responsible for its content. They felt special because we were learning with them.

Not all of the students spoke Spanish, however. I remember Ricky, a little boy in the first grade, one of two students in the class who spoke only English. He was bright and was usually interested in what we taught, but he had trouble paying attention and was usually punished by being made to sit in the back of the class. He was further isolated by his peers.

At first I didn't really like him because he seemed to act out a lot in class. When Jenny and I were teaching about owls and having the class dissect owl pellets, his interest was really sparked by a book about owls that we brought. I spent a lot of class time explaining the pictures in the book to him. He became interested and wanted to learn. I discovered how a teacher can spark interest in a student simply by showing an interest in him or her.

At the end of the year the children wrote thank-you notes to us. Their Spanish or broken English was so sweet. Jenny and I cried when we left, knowing that we would probably never get to see this group of kids again.

Dear Jenny and Janna—I joup you remember has. Thank you for chering has some roks. I am going to miss you pecous you ar, the beats. I am not going to sy you peacas I am going to Mexico to visit my family.—Love Yesenia
(Dear Jenny and Janna,—I hope you remember us. Thank you for sharing some rocks with us. I am going to miss you because you are the best. I am not going to see you because I am going to Mexico to visit my family.)

To Janna from Angel—I love you I have lurnd to not pult in mother nacher. Becous then all of the animels wiil disuper and so will we. I owe it all to you. NOT PULTE.
(...I have learned not to pollute in mother nature. Because then all of the animals will disappear and so will we... DON'T POLLUTE!)

Querida Jenny y Janna, Les quiero desir grasias por venir al clase por que ustedes ayudan an español. Les quiero desir que as ponido el corason para ayudarno. Si todavia todos los niños desimos grasias por venir a esta clase que ustedes an luchado para nosotros.—Cristina
(Dear Jenny and Janna—I want to thank you for coming to our class because you helped in Spanish. I want to tell you that you put your heart into helping us. Still all the kids want to thank you for coming to our class because you have worked for us...)

The kids we served benefited, and so did our student volunteers. Mitchie, who always wanted to be a nurse, worked as an aide at the Veterans' Hospital. She said that she made lots of friends there and felt close to her patients, but she concluded that nursing would be too demanding as a career for her. Brenda concluded the same thing about teaching. Wendy taught kids who had disabilities; she observed that some kids get labeled and lose their esteem in the process, something she vowed not to do in the profession she chooses.

Greg observed that while he taught kids about owl pellets and bird beaks, they taught him about love and generosity, and showed him how to have fun. He said, "Children make me glad to be alive." Paula, another one of our bilingual students, felt satisfaction in teaching children how to better the world by recycling and conserving water at home. Ali gained more respect for children and realized how important it was to teach them respect for the Earth. Shawn said that he felt closer to the Earth by working in a demonstration garden for children; he loved to work in the outdoors.

Andy, who taught at Peninsula School, took an interest in the class isolate. Andy got the boy interested in basketball. As the boy's self-esteem improved on the court, Andy helped transfer his interest to math in the classroom. Paki learned that, to get close to a child from a poor family, he had to accept gifts instead of giving them. Jenny learned that children respect and value teachers who reveal personal things about themselves. I re-learned that children thrive when they are drawn into the learning process. The students got more responsive as we allowed them more responsibility.

Another of our group projects was the garden project. Working in our gardens gave us a greater appreciation for the delicate balance in nature. Greg, Joanna, Andrea, and I took weekly classes at the Ecology Action/Common Ground store. Then we taught our class what we had learned. In microcosms of the world (our backyard garden sites) we applied principles of organic gardening that could be applied to the macrocosm (our Earth). We also learned that lessons appear in unexpected places in unexpected ways. This was the case, for instance, when we had to discuss commitment after Shawn, Evan, and Andrea smoked pot in the garden.

The project that touched me most deeply was the Mexicali trip. Our six-day trip to Southern California and Mexico, was prompted by our work with IDEX to support a Third World project. We had raised money to help fund the IDEX project in Mexicali, now we had to find a way to fund the trip.

Andy was our fund-raising genius for the Mexicali trip. We needed to raise $1000 to rent three vans and buy food for the group. Two fund raisers were proposed, sponsoring a dinner and putting on a talent show. We decided to do both at once. Andy volunteered to organize the dinner. He got his mom and stepfather, who are professional chefs, to volunteer to cook and serve a dinner. We organized a talent show to entertain our guests. Tamika volunteered to be the emcee for the program and perform. Greg wanted to juggle, Paki offered to play his flute, Greg and I revived our scene from *Romeo and Juliet,* Joe warmed up his sitar, and the rest of the group teamed up to write and perform a comedy. Over one-hundred people showed up to support our event, mostly family members, friends, and former Learning Community students. We reached our goal with just one activity. Then we prepared for the trip.

Our plan was to camp two nights at Joshua Tree Wilderness Reserve in southern California while en route to the farm site in Mexicali. We chose early April because that is the time of the year when the desert comes alive with greenery and colorful cacti blossoms. It is also the time between the seasons of torrential winter rains and parched summer earth.

We thrust ourselves into the austere Joshua Tree landscape. We, with our technology of pop-up tents, light-weight sleeping bags, and cooking gear, poised against nature's steep rocky mountains, unseasonably hot sun, and unseen reptiles. Our first day we got up early and watched the sun as it seemed to rise out of the sand, exposing the moonscape-like terrain. We drew deep breathes of the clean, desert air. The conditions seemed perfect for a day hike, so we tried to roust the rest of the group and start breakfast.

Wendy, Tamika, and Jenny shared a tent and shared late-night stories. They were the hardest group to roust. By the time we got everyone up, made breakfast, cleaned up, and filled dozens of water bottles, it was close to ten o'clock. By then, even the lizards were beginning to crawl under the giant boulders that covered the landscape. Our exuberant group wilted before noon. We noticed that every living creature in the desert was under the rocks. We joked about how the spirits of the indigenous Indian population were probably laughing at us as they perched *under* the big rock overhangs.

The next day, we waved our goodbyes to the Joshua Trees and continued on through the painted deserts and arid mountains of southern California. As we drew nearer to Mexico, we followed a dry riverbed into the lush green agricultural oasis of the Imperial Valley. It felt surrealistic driving through the citrus orchards after having spent three days in the desert. I also felt a sense of anticipation, knowing that Mexicali was just a few miles away. As we crossed the border into Mexico, I wondered how Wendy and Jenny felt. I knew that they had not crossed this border since their mother had brought them across illegally when they were children.

We were met at the border in Mexicali by Alonzo, our Los Niños contact in Mexico. Los Niños, a non-profit organization, had set up the garden projects and had invited us to visit the sites. They assist transient populations and seasonal workers in Mexican border communities to address health and environmental needs. Our fund-raising efforts had provided money for creating gardens at two elementary schools. The garden sites became focal points for community development. As people are brought together to plant, they talk and become acquainted. When the project is completed, people will have a base on which to further organize themselves for larger community concerns.

Our entire group had bare accommodations in an old home in a modest neighborhood near the *mercado* (market). At night the family that lived in the home fed and entertained us; we felt welcomed. We had difficulty sleeping since more than twenty of us were crowded into two rooms in the hot, sticky night heat. Los Niños arranged our daily itinerary which included going to the market, visiting a farming cooperative, discussing how development organizations help the poor, and visiting the two school sites where the demonstration gardens were located.

When we arrived at the first school, *18 de Marzo* Elementary School, I was rather shocked at the surrounding environment. The houses were dilapidated. The people lived in extremely poor conditions, poorer than anything that I had ever seen at home. Absolutely everything was covered with a layer of the thick dust that flew up from the road every time a car drove through. I didn't know what to expect from a group of children living in conditions like these.

As we entered the school yard, all the children, the teachers, and the staff lined up in front of the classrooms as if they were soldiers in the militia. The classrooms were located around a big central playground on which everyone's attention was focused. A color guard of six young girls marched out carrying the flag. One of the girls called out commands and sounded the cadence. The girls led the assembly in saluting the Mexican flag and singing the national anthem.

I was quite impressed. Here we were in the middle of a poor neighborhood watching as six uniformed girls marched in cadence while the rest of the school stood proudly in neat rows singing and saluting their flag. We were five miles from the United States border but light-years away from our culture.

After the salute, the children showed us their garden and told us about the nutrition and ecology program that had grown out of the garden project. Some of us were put to work planting *nopales* (a flat leaved cactus) with some of the kids. Then we watched a cultural show put on by the Mexican children. As a gesture of friendship, the kids gave us handcrafted gifts, drawings, and writings they had made for us.

The next day we visited Solidaridad Elementary School. Once again, we were welcomed enthusiastically. Some of the children led us to a place in which we were to draw murals. While the kids drew one for us, we drew one for them. The theme for the murals was *Kids and Ecology*. The murals were an ongoing project for the rest of the day. We had time to make friends with the kids. It was unusual for them to have visitors, so the teachers weren't very strict about keeping them in class. Some of the children took us to visit their classrooms or tour their garden.

When recess came, the rest of the students came out to play with us. Our guys teamed up with the boys to play soccer. I was mingling among a sea of children, practicing my limited Spanish here and there: "*Hola! Como te llamas?*" The children also shared soybean ceviche with us. The food is part of Los Niños' health program.

Suddenly, a little girl came up behind me and wrapped her arms around me. I turned and looked down at her; our eyes met. I don't know what it was, but for some reason, something clicked between us. We talked a little. My limited Spanish prevented any in-depth conversation, but I found out that her name was Ana and that she was six years old. We were inseparable for the rest of the day. My popularity grew as Ana and I walked around the school hand-in-hand. I developed a following of little six-year-old girls. They were excited to show me around their school.

Later in the day, I was playing volleyball with some of the older girls when Ana came up to me and asked me if she could wear my necklace. I almost started crying right there. I wanted her to have something to remember me by, so I gave the necklace. Then she went to class.

When the volleyball game ended, it was time for us to leave. I realized that recess was over and Ana was nowhere to be found. I went around looking for her but couldn't find her. I was filled by a deep sadness; it was strange. I had only met Ana earlier in the day, and yet I felt so connected to her. I couldn't imagine not seeing her again. I wanted to cry. I knew that once we left, I would never come back here. I would never see these people, this town, this school, and Ana, again.

As we made ready to leave the school, Ana came running. She took my hand and followed me to our van; then she got in with me. I sat there with her in my lap until the very last second before we had to go. I had to say "goodbye." I wanted to smile and wave as we drove away, but instead I held one hand in the air and, with the other hand, I wiped my tears away. I can't believe we made such a strong connection in such a short amount of time. I know that I'll remember her and the rest of the people I met in Mexicali for the rest of my life.

The next morning as we left Mexico and drove up the California coastal highway, thoughts of Mexicali and little Ana kept tugging at my mind. That night, we camped on the beach by the Pacific Ocean. We awoke to see dolphins swimming in the ocean just past the breaking waves. Then we drove toward home sharing thoughts of a wonderful trip.

Our final project, one that took far more time than we had ever expected, was to write a book about our experience in The Learning Community. Writing, I found, didn't always come easy. Sometimes I got frustrated when I tried to write, especially if it was something that I knew other people would read. In regular English classes, I rarely wrote about things that really mattered to me. I could always b.s. my way through papers about characters in books. It was a lot easier to write when I didn't care at all about the subject matter. Now I care because it does matter to me. I want to speak from the heart, but sometimes the words just don't come.

> *What to write? What to write? Why can't I write anything? Everyone writes such good papers. I don't know what to write about anymore. Whenever I have an idea of something I want to write about, the ideas never fall into place in the right way. No matter what I want to write about, I can never get it to sound right in my head. If I just start writing without thinking about it, letting the ideas flow, maybe I could write something worth reading. I feel as if I need to be inspired. Even when I do have a few things I'd like to write about, I just can't make them work out on paper. What to write? What to write?*

Our publishing project was a collaborative, hands-on learning project. We discussed, we planned, we organized, we wrote, and we edited. We almost bit off too much and we almost didn't come through. We wanted to write personal stories about our stages of learning and share them with others. Reflecting on our experience enabled us to see beyond ourselves.

In the end, the book project took on a life of its own, well beyond our intended deadline. It became a test for those of us who stuck with the project. It became our way to reflect, sort, evaluate, and understand the experience we created. It helped me to see learning as a moving process between people. I realized that learning is commitment, communication, collaboration, magic, and life—all at once. And as we approached the end of the year, I felt that I was inseparable from the process.

A View From the Mountain Top

Adrienne

It was the end of the school year. We were preparing to take The Learning Community final examination. It was unlike any final I had ever taken. We were asked to find a private place to sit somewhere in the classroom. Some students sprawled out on pillows on the floor; others sat against the wall, feet stretched out in front of them; some chose the couch or soft chairs around the classroom. Two richly melodic, yet ominous, compositions from Vangelis's *L'Apocalypse Des Animaux* set the mood. Gary had just guided us through a visualization in which we were to imagine ourselves in the future; we imagined living in a world that was an extrapolation of our known world. Fifty years had passed and a critical mass of people had not taken action to stop humankind from its path of social and environmental degradation. We were asked to imagine ourselves taking our grandchildren for a hike on a mountain overlooking our community. As I emerged from this closed-eye process, I began to write while "L'ours Musicien" and "Creation Du Monde" played played in the background.

My hands are old, I realize as I look down at my granddaughter's supple hand nestled in my leathered palm, our fingers of different sizes intertwined. I suppose the rest of me is old as well. The whole world feels old in fact. The people seem just to settle for the status quo and to lack energy or passion to try to change things. And a lot needs to change.

As I hike up this mountain, child at my side, I think back to the Saturdays I spent planting and caring for the oak trees in these foothills when I was young. On a clear day I could see the entire valley and the buildings in downtown San Francisco in the distance. Smog that once hovered only over San Jose and the Silicon Valley has become dense and now engulfs all of the Bay Area. It is as if someone has poured a thick, brown layer of spoiled milk into this valley up to the tips of the surrounding hills and mountains. Oh, and the smell. The whiff of exhaust emission that I occasionally caught when stuck behind an old car or diesel truck is now the typical smell of a hot day.

Human impact on the land astounds me once again. As if there are no limits, we have crowded the hills and mountains with our many possessions and houses, creating a suburban sprawl that encompasses the valley. This valley, which my grandfather remembered as more crowded with plum and apricot orchards than people, now explodes with people and their cars. Thick, dirty air parches my throat as my granddaughter and I gasp for breath.

Tears begin to cloud my eyes and I bite my lip, hoping my granddaughter will not sense my despair on this special occasion. This is not the world I would like to live in. Where did we go wrong, I ask myself. How could we have let the world come to this?

A gentle breeze raises the wisps of my granddaughter's dark hair off her shoulders and reminds me that it is springtime. I forget easily because there are no flowers around us. I almost overlook the absence of native plants because it has been so long since I have seen the purple lupine and soap plant. They disappeared after a long battle with non-native grasses introduced by the Spanish. The Spanish first brought cattle to this area over 200 years ago, initiating a process of soil degradation and mineral depletion leading to loss of the beautiful California Oak. Many species no longer exist and I know that my granddaughter will know about them only through the memories I share with her. At home we no longer have squirrels or birds; the only animals around are stray scavenger dogs. Most children grow up so distant from nature and animals that their concept of the world includes only people and the artifacts that people have created.

I envision myself among the people and buildings in the landscape below. I often move deftly among them, preoccupied with a sense of loneliness and fear. I rarely interact with strangers during the day; computers have reduced human interaction and the world seems increasingly impersonal. Sometimes I feel like a consumer-pawn of the corporate and political "powers that be." Advertisements bombard me daily and I begin to doubt whether my existence matters at all besides my worth as a consumer. Each day the newspapers glorify the latest fad or report political demise. I search for meaningful experiences and moments in this external world, but everything seems reduced to simplicity. It is so much easier to hide than to face this desperate world we have created. I look into my granddaughter's deep brown eyes and wonder how she can survive in this world that desensitizes us more each day. I hope that my love will help make her strong enough to see beyond. But what about everyone else?

We gaze out at all the people living in our area and I wonder what price we will have to pay for exceeding the carrying-capacity of the region. The concentration of wealth for the few still makes this country the richest country in the world; yet our needs and material desires depend on the exploitation of resources from far-away places. And the majority in our country is miserable. We are, indubitably, paying the price. As a society, as well as individually, we suffer more now than ever before. People seem to be driven by an artificial desire to achieve material wealth as they have been for years, but wealth is far more unattainable than before because we live in a regimented society with a class system determined by birth, race, and gender. Personal freedom is tremendously restricted. When I walk through the city, I see troops stationed in an attempt to curb violence—violence that has festered because society has failed to provide support and healthy stimulation for its disillusioned youth.

Poverty, which was so long ignored in America, now affects everyone. Thousands live in perpetual poverty and everyone seems faced with losing everything in an age of such economic instability. Companies merge and downsize daily resulting in fewer jobs. Slums, like the favelas that surrounded Rio de Janerio, Brazil, seventy-five years ago and that we never thought would exist in America, now encompass almost every major city. These slums consist of people living in overcrowded shacks constructed desperately out of cardboard and scrap tin. Rats and disease are everywhere. People collect paper and scraps to make enough money to feed their families.

I look down at my hands, feeling lucky that, after striving for a good education, I found a good job and managed to live in a small house. But I could not escape all pain. As I run the fingers of my right hand over the back of my left hand, I wince at the open pustules and cracked skin, skin cancer caused by ultraviolet rays more intense than ever. Cancer seems to afflict everyone, analogous, I suppose, to the cancer we have inflicted upon the earth.

The only good thing, if one took a very global position, is that the population is decreasing. The death rate exceeds the birth rate due to rampant disease—a phenomena that baffled scientists fifty years ago when they discovered that Russians were dying younger than in any other industrialized nation and that each year their life spans were decreasing even more for no known reason. Our *own government ignored the decrease in global population when it afflicted the rest of the world fearing that it might cause wide-spread panic.*

Globally we face a food shortage owing to the loss of commercial food crops to chemically resistant bacteria and insects. The lack of biodiversity in agriculture has also wiped out the huge meat-producing ranches upon which industrialized nations had become dependent. The economies of many industrialized nations have become less stable than they once were because of their heavy dependence on imported resources and fossil fuels.

Biologically, microorganisms are threatening the human race. Bacteria, which can reproduce and alter genetically thousands of times faster than humans, have rendered almost all antibiotics and vaccinations useless. However, merely to say that the population declines, turns suffering into a statistic. Disease spreads like wildfire. I hear of families that are torn apart as districts impose quarantines in attempt to isolate diseases. Some of my family members and friends have died suddenly of "unknown causes." Even the illusion of certainty and security no longer exists.

And as I look out at a valley of festering filth, I feel it in myself. Facets of life seem disconnected, and within I feel detached, distraught, despairing. My addictions have manifested in areas of working and running, things which can be healthy when done in a conscious manner. But these activities have become crutches for me to survive at a speedy pace of life. In public interactions I feel a numbness—a loss of hope and camaraderie. Like others, I carry fear and have learned to avoid eye contact and exchanges of genuine compassion. When I walk the streets, I feel alone. Despite our common suffering, I no longer feel a common bond with humanity.

As my granddaughter and I gaze out at the world, my fear mounts. I feel the pain of all life as my own. As I feel my granddaughter's hand resting trustfully in mine, I experience total realization of my own actions and of the actions of those around me and the fear inebriates my entire body. I am fully accountable for this dearth and utter deterioration of all life.

Suddenly the child at my side breaks the silence with one of those direct, penetrating questions children are prone to ask adults that shake our world of obfuscation and delusion. "Why is it so ugly?" she inquires.

Her question strikes the nerve of acute pain I try to protect. I wonder how I can explain that my peers and I were simply too short-sighted to leave her anything better. How can I explain that fifty years ago, at the end of the millennium, when we needed a critical mass of people to commit to making the world a better place, that a critical mass failed to emerge. And how can I explain that, although I felt that I cared, my actions resulted in this world because I also remained passive.

Suddenly I am brought back into the classroom as Gary guides us out of the meditation and asks us to regroup and share our worst-possible future scenarios. Thankfully, I do not need to explain my visualization to my granddaughter or to the rest of humanity. This powerful image is a reminder; a prophecy of our future if we do not alter the course right now. I leave that world, which seems all too real, and turn to familiar faces, faces that give me hope, for they too have learned by seeing into the horrors.

After writing our reflections on our experiences with our grandchild, Gary asked us to close our eyes and relax, get into a comfortable position, and prepare for another guided visualization. We were asked to imagine that we had just returned home from our hike on the mountain. We had taken our grandchild home, returned to our home, and found a special letter addressed to us containing a summons which said:

As a respected citizen of planet Earth in the year 2050, you are summoned by the president of the League of Global Citizens to an emergency meeting of the Global Council of Twenty-Five. It has been determined that the vital triangle of life—physical health, social well being, and environmental harmony—has become dramatically threatened and is in acute danger of falling into irreparable destruction. It is feared that these circumstances may result in a serious degradation of life or even the extinction of human life on the planet.

You have been chosen to be a member of the Council because of your commitment to the well-being of all life forms on the planet, and because you have maintained a thorough and continuing knowledge of planetary issues over the past fifty years.

Gary asked us to imagine ourselves packing our bags, being transported to the airport, and beginning our flight to Geneva, Switzerland. On the plane ride, we were to consider what global solution we might have to share with other people of the world. We were also to think about the personal strengths that we had cultivated over our lifetimes to prepare ourselves educationally and professionally for this calling. The music of Vangelis—"Le Singe Bleu" and "La Mort Du Loup"—permeated my thoughts as I imagined what I might have accomplished over the past fifty years.

In spite of the general apathy in the society, I devoted much of my energy building bridges between disparate groups and bringing people together to solve social and environmental problems. My education and experience as an activist helped me gain communication skills for mediating conflicts and striving for solutions that worked for everyone rather than decisions that created winners and losers. I became involved in policy building regarding environmental issues from logging to implications of the Endangered Species Act on private property. I also worked with neighborhood communities to restructure education to better meet the needs of students and the changing world, sometimes helping to build exciting partnerships between corporations and classrooms. Often, I felt discouraged because the general population was too engrossed in material things and pleasure seeking to notice that something needed to be done to protect society. As societal conditions worsened, people became even more greedy and self-serving.

After taking time to reflect on what our personal lives may have been, we continued our guided visualization:

Imagine that you have arrived at your destination. An official of The League of Global Citizens meets you at the airport. As you drive through the streets of Geneva, you recall your visit to the city as a youthful traveler during college.

Every aspect of the city shows the effects of fifty years of societal neglect. Now you are the hope of the future.

Then we opened our eyes and began a simulation of the *Council of Twenty-Five*. Gary read the welcoming introduction:

The Council of Twenty-Five will convene shortly. After you have introduced yourselves to other members of the Council, you are to define together the problems facing our planet. You are to identify, describe, and prioritize these problems by degrees of severity. Then you are to create a comprehensive global solution to five of the problems you have singled out as the most serious.

In addition, each member of the Council will commit to a set of specific actions in his/her life that will make a difference in the world. The specific actions should include both changes in the member's personal lifestyle and professional contributions.

The process became more personal as each of us imagined what our lives might become in the next fifty years. These imagined outcomes took form as we interacted as if we had just met for the first time in the Council of Twenty-five. The roles gave each of us a credible position of expertise on the Council. As experts with a wealth of experience and a global perspective, we had been summoned to assess areas of world crisis and propose solutions to the problems we identified. Our roles reflected our unique interests and talents.

Tamika, the civil rights lawyer, had devoted her life to challenging individuals and corporations that breached or impinged upon the rights of others. She had set up a non-profit foundation that provided homes and educational alternatives for inner city kids.

Jeremy had used his influence as a successful corporate CEO to write and promote an Ethical Practices Pledge which several major corporations had agreed upon. The Pledge provided that corporations would pursue more healthy, humane, and ecological practices in bringing their product to market.

Greg had become known as the Zen Master Harlequin and traveled all over the world giving performances. He had an array of masks that helped him portray ways of being in the world. His performances were engaging and humorous, but, more than that, they helped transform the awareness of the audience.

Shawn, the truck driver who had gotten skin cancer from exposure to the environment, had turned his solar-powered trucking company into an advertisement on wheels. From coast to coast, people could read posters on his big-rig trucks that warned of environmental health risks and supported political solutions. His enterprise hauled only products that were environmentally safe.

Jenny had graduated from the university in International Relations. She had helped develop a non-governmentally sustained organization that support landless people in Central America. She gained financial support for her projects by writing books, giving public lectures, appealing to people's altruism.

Kristie worked as a wildlife biologist in the northern Rockies. She was an advocate for Natural Habitat Zones. These were regions in which people using only passive forms of energy and practicing sound environmental principles could live in forested watershed preserves.

Angel had used her song writing talent and her voice to gain support for interfaith conferences. Attendees shared in one another's spiritual celebrations, performed inspirational music, and funded grass-roots social action proposals.

Janna had helped establish a set of charter schools across the country that were governed democratically by their students, staff, and parents. Graduates of her schools were known for their compassion and activism. Some of her graduates were carrying on the tradition of establishing activist schools.

Each of the other students in the class created a role for him or herself. Andrea had helped encourage a regional interest in growing nutritional and healing herbs in hydroponic gardens. Wendy had become a social worker who pioneered systems for ending the need for welfare. Joe had set up urban homesteading projects after studying effective practices around the world. Julie had set up international conflict resolution teams to serve regions of the world which were in turmoil. Each student linked his or her core interest to some need in the world, then extrapolated a life of service around that interest. As experts with a wealth of experience and global perspective about the state of the world, we talked.

Each of us shared our concerns about the world and offered major issues to be considered by the group. Some students addressed health issues: water pollution, lack of good nutrition, the failure of infectious disease control, and dependency on alcohol, drugs, and tobacco. Some students addressed social issues: teenage suicide and alienation; social issues such as abortion, crime prevention, rehabilitation, and the death penalty; rape, genital mutilation, and other crimes against women; racial prejudice and inclusion; political oppression and treatment of political prisoners; the effects of imperialism and war on indigenous people; and the fair distribution of the world's resources. Other students addressed environmental issues: effects of pesticides on the ecology; ozone depletion and global warming; protection of endangered species; threat of nuclear energy and weapons. One issue seemed to fit in all three categories: the effects of over-population.

In our roles we faced many of the struggles that diplomats face trying to formulate and apply international policy. Sometimes the group process became frustrating. We felt that it was absolutely essential that everyone take the initiative to speak and that the group respect every idea. Our process of sharing our career paths and our major issues was exciting and infused high level energy into our group. However, when we attempted to sort out, to prioritize, and to find solutions to the issues, we fell into confusion and disunity. I wanted things to work out. I wanted our year to end in great harmony and be perfect, but our experience showed me just how thin the veneer of civility can be.

We finally agreed on a fairly universal approach to the problems that faced us. The solutions were broad and long-term. We saw the value of public education programs which emphasized the arts in communicating global messages. We saw the value of community-based partnerships which brought citizens, industry, and government together to solve problems. We agreed on the value of encouraging individual choices in selecting products and food and in using resources and eliminating waste. We realized that governments could provide laws and regulations but that people had to be committed to outcomes in order for real change to occur.

Then we jumped out of our roles as citizens of the year 2050. For some it was the first time for envisioning the future, picturing oneself in the grand scheme, and committing to a solution. We made lifestyle commitments affecting our current lives. Shawn agreed to recycle at home, at school, and in the community. Brenda agreed to volunteer to help in a community health abuse program. Andy agreed to work in local environmental clean-up projects. Personally, I felt that, in the process, I reaffirmed my responsibility to take a positive role in the evolution of the planet.

Sometimes the group strayed from the focus and debated trivial details. When Andrea proposed ways she would change her actions she said she would stop using the clothes dryer and the microwave. We discussed the potential energy conservation benefits and dangers, and, unable to come to a decision about microwaves, we concluded that it is imperative that people be educated so they can make conscious decisions about their actions.

My level of personal optimism ebbed and flowed. Sometimes I doubted the sincerity of our group's commitment. I wondered if people felt obligated to say something or if they were saying things that sounded nice. I do not give much credit to words or promises, perhaps because I don't trust my own words. In my life, I need to see action and I need to live my values. As I sat there listening to my peers speak, I wondered why I felt such distrust in my own words. I thought about my childhood:

> *I was an extremely quiet child and my mother used to wonder why I did not play with the other kids at the playground. My mother decided that I should be exposed to more adults when I was young so that I would not become dependent on her and she would not be an overbearing force in my life. So,*

early on she went off to work and I was shipped off to day care centers. I think that leaving so abruptly probably affected me a lot and created a distrust. In a sense it severed our bond. Fortunately, I ended up at a nurturing school—Peninsula—where I had met Kristie, and gradually engaged in play with the other children and became more assertive. But again my security was shattered when my parents sent me to public school at the end of the fifth grade. They wanted me to be academically prepared for public high school. I remember the day they told me I was changing schools. I was to leave my extended family. The little girl in me was so devastated. At the new school people didn't care about each other in the way that I had grown accustomed. To make matters worse, I was confronted with an emphasis on right and wrong, rather than on learning.

Then Jenny spoke and I redirected my attention back to the group. Jenny always spoke consciously, and I knew that I could trust her. Our group process continued and we eventually arrived at consensus on certain goals. Then we concluded our four-hour final with another guided visualization accompanied by music. I assumed a comfortable position on the floor, closed my eyes and relaxed. Gary asked us to repeat the walk up the mountain with our grandchildren. This time we were to view a world in which a critical mass of people *had taken* responsibility for the vital triangle of life. We had learned the lessons of balancing personal power with responsibility, balancing group action with harmony, and balancing our use of the planet with care for the environment.

As the music of Vangelis's "La Mer Recommencee" blended with my thoughts, I imagined smelling the freshness of the air, seeing the beauty of the flowers, and hearing the songs of the birds as we ascended the mountain. This time, I could point out to my grandchild all the things that I had helped to create in the world over my lifetime. Now I could talk about the health of the people, the cooperative spirit of the citizenry, the vitality of the land, the plants, and the animals. I began to envision the world as it could be if a critical mass had emerged and empowered themselves to make a difference.

My granddaughter holds my hand in hers as we move up the mountain in silence, mindful of each footstep and aware of our surroundings. She moves with natural grace, communicating a sort of old familiarity with the outdoors and respect for the sacredness as she carefully examines the life we are among. Sometimes we just stop to observe and experience the movement of a creature or the stillness of a tree. We are gentle with one another in our touch and with our words. We have traveled this mountain many times—sometimes alone, sometimes guided by others, sometimes ascending in harmony guided by a common vision and loving one another.

The air is clear and a zephyr rustles the leaves on the trees. When we stop to gaze out at the valley I feel connected to the movement below. I know that beneath us people have come together in a common venture to improve life and the environment. People have learned, for the most part, to identify with a global community and see the need to work together rather than compete. At some point in many people's lives, their care manifested into action and like a drop in a pool the active energy of this change rippled out and affected a change within the hearts of others.

More and more individuals became mindful of the way they consumed both natural resources and the energy around them and directed their energy in unique ways to create a healthier community. Recognizing that individuals shape and are shaped by the institutions we create, some committed to making institutions such as schools, government, and business more humane.

Small changes in living brought about dramatic change in the environment. Having long been aware of pesticide contamination of water and potential health dangers, people truly committed to buying local, organic produce and created gardens in the cities and suburbs. Many found ways to live more simply and to do their own household tasks reducing the class division exacerbated by the sort of domestic servitude common in some suburbs. People chose to live closer together, creating dense pockets of population and strong communities and preserving open space. Living in close quarters, people naturally joined together for community events, shared or traded their resources, and chose to bicycle or use mass transit.

I remember the point at which I realized that every one of my actions and every moment of my life must be directed toward creating a better world. My life was transformed. Suddenly the way that I got to my destination and my experience along the way became as important and invigorating as the rest of my life. Getting somewhere in a hurry or spending the journey distracted by my racing thoughts or the radio no longer felt satisfying. I renounced my car for the fresh air of a bike ride or walk to work or the smile and conversation with a stranger on the train. I became even more scrupulous about what I consumed, both internally and externally.

I removed myself from situations that were not in accordance with my vision and I directed my energy towards actions that would open me and those around me towards freedom. I strove to live every moment with openness, with exhilaration as if it were my first and exaltation as if it were my last. With each action I tried to consider if I would like to live in a world in which everyone was acting as I was in that moment. Gradually I learned that I could act mindfully, without imposing rules and restrictions on myself. As I began to meditate and find inner peace, my choices were guided by a wise inner voice that felt natural and joyful.

Then we took time to share our visualizations. Tamika shared a common frustration: it was easier to imagine and write about the most negative of futures; it was harder to imagine and write about a positive future. As we shared our visualizations, I realized that we shared a common fear. We feared that we might live in a world where people did not care about one another, about the environment, or about humanity as a whole. I felt discouraged: here we had spent the year together, found trust and love in ourselves and one another, and learned to see the world in a larger context and care for it, and yet we did not see it in our future that people would care.

Frustration swelled within me as I forced myself to step back and reflect further. I relaxed as I inferred that it did not appear that we had lost faith in humanity. We did not view humans as malicious or vindictive. Instead we envisioned a passive fate. We saw people caught up in materialism and becoming numb to an innate sense of oneness with the world. Perhaps we feared this most because we saw it in ourselves. We were in our visions of the world at its worst and we were culpable merely by being passive.

Throughout my life my parents had high standards for my behavior. When they saw me making decisions that took me away from my studies and toward my friends, they threatened to take away things that I cherished— even The Learning Community. They wanted me to do well in college and feared that I would not be prepared. My parents took note of how miserable I was and realized the delicate balance inherent in my social and academic development. Still, I was frightened and confused. I became insecure, feeling that everything is transient and nothing is mine because things and privileges were constantly being taken away. I suppose I figured out early on that if I couldn't trust the people around me, I couldn't trust myself. As I grappled with my frustrations I realized that some of my childhood scars had followed me here.

Then Gary asked that we close by writing a reflection of our day. As Vangelis played "La Petite Fille De Lamar," I couldn't help but to reflect on my entire year. I looked around the circle and I saw individual faces. I looked into the eyes of people who had committed to the group—who had committed to me. We had shared an incredible year. These people had not let me down. When it mattered the most we had been here for each other. We were a group, a unit, a family. I thought about the instances in which people had emerged as warriors—Tamika in her struggle with the sadness and trauma of her childhood, Greg in bringing us back to the heart of an issue and back to our own hearts, showing us gently and by example how to care for each other, Wendy in standing up to Shawn and Jeremy with such honest passion.

And as I saw each person again, I saw the individual strengths that had emerged over the year through love and support. Kristie had really recognized her intellectual potential and become more assertive. Angel had come out of her own world, joined the circle instead of disrupting it, and, as she committed her energy to the group, contributed incredible insight.

I looked around the circle again. This group had supported me fully when I had been weak and struggled against my own inhibitions and when I had been strong and taken risks emerging as a leader in the group. And I remembered how each of these beautiful people had touched me so deeply in life outside the group: Kristie being so honest and open; Wendy being with me one afternoon and just holding me when things had been so hard at home; and Steve magically bringing out my laughter and love and helping me to dance. We were a group, a unit; this was my family away from home.

As I looked at everyone I realized that I had a special relationship with each person in the group. I felt their love, and in that moment, trusting the group, I trusted myself. I thought of a Taoist story that Gary had shared with us about a farmer who, in his desire to help his plants grow, went into his fields each day gently pulling on each seedling; and how the farmer inadvertently killed his plants by rushing their growth process. We can love and nurture each other while we each develop and learn in our inherently natural way.

I realized that nothing in an individual's education could be more important and relevant than the process we were engaged in: recognizing our potential, liberating ourselves to become the learners we wanted to become with the support of a group, and becoming inspired to take an active part in the conscious evolution of the planet.

Yes, I thought, education is stepping outside oneself and connecting with humanity through literature and history; it is learning by experimenting—the process of science and math; it is being in nature and feeling the connection between oneself and all of life; it is interacting with others and learning to share and to love; and it is the vital step in which all of this culminates into action. It is recognizing that the state of humanity and our environment depends on how we act and interact right now. And it is this process over and over again within the individual and within a group. As I made my personal commitment to work actively to improve my community and the environment, I let go and allowed myself to trust the group and in doing so I liberated myself.

Our learning community started out as a group of diverse personalities. We were separate as boys and girls and we were made even more separate by being regarded as freshmen, sophomores, juniors, and seniors. We experienced, interacted, became aware, and agreed to seek the higher intellectual ground in arguments. We re-directed our focus from self-indulgence and the confrontation that produces winners and losers; we transformed "my concerns" to "our concerns" to "global concerns."

As the year ends, we take the awareness that we had worked so hard to transform and prepare ourselves for the next step: to walk alone once again into the world and face the challenges that our lives presented. We are ready to create our future. We need more education and more experience, and we need to create opportunities in which to become involved and bring our new consciousness into action.

I carry all these thoughts with me as I begin my new journey alone. The process makes me both excited and afraid. I am left with questions: Will I be able to live up to the challenge? Will I find others who will join me in setting their differences aside and commit to common causes? Will we be able to make a difference? I don't know the answers; sometimes I feel overwhelmed by the questions.

I know that at times I will be filled with loneliness and doubt. And I know that at other times I will be excited and uplifted by the optimistic spirit and the camaraderie that I will share with others. I know that when I open myself to my greatest vision of the future, I am energized and feel totally alive. I have control over my willingness to help create a better world and I intend to exercise that control. It is the only certainty that I have.

Afterthought

Over the course of the history of American public education, generations of sincere and dedicated people have worked hard to create a school system that reflects everything that western civilization has to offer. The efforts of professional educators to perfect the system, coupled with the public's demand for more from its institutions, have resulted in a complex, highly organized and structured system that monopolizes the life of young Americans from pre-adolescence to adulthood.

During the same historical period, American society has undergone enormous changes. The industrial revolution changed the face of the country and its schools as a rural America gave way to an urban America. We have witnessed accelerated change in our own lifetimes as the industrial revolution has been replaced by the information age, spawning a high-tech information-oriented society.

Visionaries are now making a convincing case that the information age is giving way to an even more critical period for the human species, the consciousness age. They claim that we are at a critical juncture for human survival in which we have the opportunity to develop a harmonious planetary consciousness to guide us into the future. The schools are the logical institutions in which this new consciousness can be explored and developed. All the well-intended efforts by the schools will provide little comfort if our life-supporting infrastructure collapses. An enlightened educational community and an enlightened public is needed to reverse the trend toward social and environmental degradation that is threatening the planet.

But change comes slowly in an education system that is guided by antiquated and incomplete paradigms. Unfortunately, old paradigms die slowly and, if they die too slowly, they take their adherents and the systems they created with them. Public education could lose the public's support or die, if it does not change to meet the demands of a rapidly changing world. The structure of the old way of educating — including its weighty curriculum, teacher-centered methodology, territorial politics, hierarchical management, and university-driven standards — must be radically changed to make room for real and effective education.

It is unlikely that the new way will be forged by those who have vested interests in the old way — people rarely let go of their power bases. Nor is it likely that the new way will be forged with curriculum mandates that favor content over process — information acquisition alone deadens the human spirit and stifles innovation. The new way will never be forged by people clinging to the limited educational view that stops at basic skills development, vocational training, or inculcation of the majority culture — the effective educator needs a world view that recognizes the transformational aspect of human consciousness.

We wish to join you in a continuing search for a new educational paradigm. You have read the accompanying passages characterizing our award-winning approach to learning and human understanding. Our program is an open system that has successfully adapted to change over a twenty-five year period and remains vital today. Through our true accounts, you have seen how the development of the whole person energizes the heart of education; you have seen the richness that manifests when learners are included in the developmental process; and you have seen how beneficial and rewarding a global approach to education is for young people, and how it leads, naturally, to social and environmental service. Take what you want from these experiences; then take what you know — in your heart — and continue to help forge the new way in education.

Gary Bacon April 7, 1997